FLASHBACKS

THE FLASHBACKS SERIES IS PUBLISHED BY THE
EUROPEAN ETHNOLOGICAL RESEARCH CENTRE
CELTIC & SCOTTISH STUDIES
UNIVERSITY OF EDINBURGH
50 GEORGE SQUARE
EDINBURGH EH8 9LH

FLASHBACKS

Going to the Berries

Voices of Perthshire and Angus Seasonal Workers

Written by
Roger Leitch

Edited by
Caroline Milligan

in association with
THE EUROPEAN ETHNOLOGICAL RESEARCH CENTRE
AND NMS ENTERPRISES LIMITED – PUBLISHING
NATIONAL MUSEUMS SCOTLAND

GENERAL EDITOR
Mark A. Mulhern

Co-published in Great Britain
in 2020 by
NMS Enterprises Limited – Publishing
National Museums Scotland
Chambers Street
Edinburgh EH1 1JF

and the
European Ethnological Research Centre
Celtic & Scottish Studies
University of Edinburgh
50 George Square
Edinburgh EH8 9LH

ISBN 978-1-910682-39-5

The right of Roger Leitch to be identified
as the author of this book has been
asserted by him in accordance with the
Copyright, Designs and Patents Act 1988.

**British Library Cataloguing in
Publication Data**

A catalogue record of this book is
available from the British Library.

Cover design by Mark Blackadder.
Cover photograph: Gothens Farm,
    weighing station, 1962, left to right:
    John Hodge (payclerk), Jock Morton
    (grieve), Martin Doherty and Will
    Crighton. (Hodge archive).

Internal text design by
    NMS Enterprises Ltd – Publishing.
Printed and bound in Great Britain by
    Bell & Bain Ltd, Glasgow.

For a full listing of related NMS titles
please visit:
www.nms.ac.uk/books

CONTENTS

ACKNOWLEDGEMENTS

Firstly, a special debt of gratitude is due R. D. Soutar who supplied me with a range of printed matter from recycled newspapers to local history scrapbooks. Since I was not online, these aided preparation for interviews and endnotes. The Craigie column in *The Courier* was especially helpful.

Andrew Hodge generously put his grandfather's archival collection at my disposal and secured oral history contributors for me in the Blairgowrie area.

Empirical fieldwork with folklorist Donald Archie Mac-Donald in the Uists was of tremendous value. Sylvia Robertson kindly shared details derived from school logbooks. Ishbel Mac-Leod and her husband, the Revd Murdo MacLeod, gave of their time to translate life story material of Peter Morrison from his book, *Ugam Agus Bhuam*.

Friends became contributors. Three of whom are sadly missed: former brickie, gaffer and site agent, Chic Milne (93) and his son, Charlie, who died in just over a year of each other. The late Helen Jackson, latterly a schoolteacher at Kilgraston, was outstanding. As an author and local historian, Helen helped put Niel Gow and Beatrix Potter on the map of Highland Perthshire. Dementia in the end destroyed her memory but she lived to a fortnight short of her 100th birthday, in 2015.

Friends from way back helped out too: Brian Melville of Oxford, Mike Macfarlane when home from Michigan, USA,

Martin Anderson and Iain Smart, who was as steady as a rock – just as he had been in our winter mountaineering days.

Without bus drivers, Scotrail and truckers, I would not have travelled as far afield. I was also fortunate to have friends who eased travel with lifts: included in my gratitude are the late Bill Kidd of Lower Largo; John Robb; Willie Duncan, a time-served pattern-maker and Bill Reid, formerly of Central Farmers. The congenial Brendan Coleman from Dublin also took me most of the way on my first field trip to Dumfries and Galloway, translated Irish Gaelic and one Christmas filled up my fridge and freezer with food.

Postbuses were also a lifeline in remote areas. Hitchhiking was more possible then and on one coastal odyssey en route to Troon, Steve Turnbull and I had our ninth and final lift courtesy of an empty hearse.

Sales engineer and entrepreneur, John H. Beaton MBE, was a pivotal contributor and contact man. Irene Cumming, the former Tayside Police events organiser, introduced me to Willie Mac-Farlane, curator of the Tayside Police Museum, and his former colleague, Andy McKay.

I was fortunate and privileged to record traditional singers, the late Sheila Stewart MBE, and Sheena Wellington.

There would be no book without the many other contributors represented here. The former Children 1st Charity shop was a regular and joyous destination on many Friday mornings. I am especially grateful to managers, Diane Donnelly and Anne Piggott, plus volunteers, Moyra Carr, the effervescent Anne McDonald (née Egan), Mary Angus and Maureen Gardiner.

A quartet from the world of health and social care who turned lives around for the better and assisted my research were Jennifer Burns, Joan Kettles, Irene Lodge and Margaret McMaster. These ladies were gems who also provided nuggets of personal life experience.

Collecting printed sources without the help of booksellers would have been far more difficult and far less enjoyable. For their kindness and professionalism, I am grateful to the generosity of Bill Anderson (Bouquiniste), Sheila and Alan Clubb (formerly Brand's Books, Stobswell), the late Douglas Hill, Gordon Dow and Mike Moir (Oxfam), Kenny MacLeod, Frank Mills (of the wonderful Groucho's record shop) and Alan Wilkes. A special indebtedness is due to former bookseller and librarian, Ian Anderson of Gribton, Dumfries.

Back newspapers were searched with grateful respect to the journalists, and efficiency and diligence of librarians at the A. K. Bell Library, Perth, and Dundee Central Library. Archival research was exciting and it was a pleasure to be directed by Caroline Brown and Dr Jan Merchant (University of Dundee), Dr Iain Flett and Richard Cullen (Dundee City Council), Steve Connelly and Ishbel MacKinnon (Perth & Kinross), Dr Alan Bruford and Dr Cathlin Macaulay (School of Scottish Studies). All are owed a big thank you.

Tony Brenchley in East Anglia and Jim Page were valiant allies concerning the Caledonian Railway Company's local history in the Blairgowrie area. Their output is railway scholarship of a high quality and deserves wider recognition.

I was inspired by academics such as the late Professor J. B. Caird, Professor Alexander 'Sandy' Fenton, Dr Hamish Henderson, Professor John 'Jack' MacQueen, J. J. Robertson and Dr Bruce Walker.

The late Iain MacRae of Torridon and the prolific oral historian Ian MacDougall gave me encouragement and vital fillips when morale dipped, as did the much missed Beth Mollison, who fell victim to multiple sclerosis. Ian MacRae introduced me to Angus Morrison of Scalpay who had a near photographic memory. Also, at the former Sandeman Library, Perth, I had the pleasure of working with talented people as part of an oral history project. Dennis Buchan and Ian Haddow helped sow the seeds of this. But all were stars including Patricia Anderson, Angela Comer, Malcolm Dodds, Andy Marnock and Ann Wishart.

Dr Ian Francis helped out at times when I was on my 'uppers' as a student. I had numerous jobs that were a real 'university of life'. This book was aided by sound folk from the wider community, without whom I could not have managed; namely Andy and Heather Anderson, Gavin A. Cook, Ian and Lee Dunbar, Bob Fotheringham, Mike Henderson, Paul Hill, John Jordan, David Leggat, John MacKenzie, Neil Martin, Ron Morris, Ian and Sybil Murray, Andra Noble, Loraine Noble, Scott Roberts, Alistair L. Strachan, Dean Tait, Mark and Richard Urban, David and Mairi Wilson.

Practical tools in the form of cassette tapes and stationery came from Tesco Dundee Riverside, as well as fairly priced photocopying at Urban Print, thanks to Frank and Carole Urban.

Being left last by no means is least. The acknowledgements are often the hardest part of a book to get right. Those that I have omitted are by error and lack of space.

A huge debt of thanks is due to Caroline Milligan who had to persevere with my handwriting and to the series editor, Mark A. Mulhern. To Professor Gary West and staff at Celtic and Scottish Studies, and the EERC, a special thank you is well deserved.

At the end of the day the project and book owes everything to the people who took part. Thanks are given here to all those who have generously shared their time and their memories with me. I hope they will be pleased with the fruits of our joint labours and that they and their families will be happy with the record we have created together.

Roger Leitch
Dundee

LIST OF ILLUSTRATIONS

INTRODUCTION

L ike many with an interest in ethnology and oral history I was
 aware of Roger Leitch's earlier publications, most particularly
his study, *The Book of Sandy Stewart*, which was published in 1988.
This work told the story, through oral history and photographs, of
the lives of Scottish Traveller Sandy Stewart, his wife Peggie and
their sons Davie and Sandy. *The Book of Sandy Stewart* is a key text
for students of the discipline for both its content and methodology
and it remains as relevant today as it was when it was first published.

Although based primarily on fieldwork recordings gathered
more recently in Dundee and Blairgowrie, this publication is also
a reflection of Roger's life as an ethnologist and so in chapter 1
Roger shares recollections with us from a career immersed in
ethnological fieldwork study. We learn that he first encountered
ethnology when he came to study within the History Department
at the University of Edinburgh. One of the lectures he attended
was taught by Dr Eric Cregeen, of the School of Scottish Studies.
Eric illustrated his talk with excerpts from a recording he had made
of two old men on Mull and that first experience of an ethnological
field-recording was to be a turning point for Roger: 'Oral history
had colour and vibrancy and provided a link with humanity in a
way that no other subject had previously achieved for me. I was
hooked'. He immediately embarked on fieldwork recording and
subsequently transferred to the School of Scottish Studies where
he immersed himself in their sound archive collection whilst

continuing to make fieldwork recordings himself.

What strikes me when I read about Roger's development as an ethnologist is the joy which is imbued in his crystal clear memories of individual fieldwork encounters. In essence, ethnological or oral history fieldwork is about gathering information on our shared cultural life through first hand experiences. But it is also a meeting, a conversation, and a unique experience for the participants. For the researcher who later listens to a fieldwork interview, oral history can provide an opportunity to make an authentic reconnection to a different place and time. For the fieldworker that moment in time is often very special. We glimpse this in Roger's encounter with Wull and Violet Halliday of Meikle Kirkland. As he recalls:

> Violet, Wull's wife, had lit the coal fire and produced a marvellous spread for my visit. As the tape rolled Wull told me that it was his aunt, Sarah, who had passed the family stories on to him. Her father had been 'born on the nicht o Waterloo', Wull recalled. There was thus an unbroken passage of almost 170 years in family tradition and I felt privileged that he shared his time and history with me. ... I left Wull feeling buoyed by our encounter. I found him and his way of life enriching and truly special.

Through Roger's fieldwork recollections there emerges a real sense of what it is to be an ethnologist. In this chapter we also learn about how fieldwork practice has changed over time. One of the key impacts on practice has been with the recording machines themselves. Roger's own fieldwork experience dates to a time when a battery-operated Uher device, which used small open-reel tapes, could be easily transported in a small bag. But he also considers earlier times when recordings were made onto wax cylinders or open-reel machines which were extremely heavy and often required external microphones and huge batteries or an electrical supply. The recording equipment always has an impact on the recording space dynamic and the size and type of machine influences this to a greater or lesser extent. In current practice, a small recording device can be an almost imperceptible presence and this presents its own challenges for the ethnologist.

There is information here too about the day-to-day life of an ethnologist and through this account we can appreciate why Roger has developed his commitment to oral history. For him it is the best method for exploring, learning about and then sharing our collective history. What is also evident in this chapter is that throughout his career Roger has been collecting material about the themes which are central to this publication: people living close to the land or coast and travelling through the landscape, often in pursuit of rural seasonal labour.

Roger's fieldwork collection includes many recordings relating to a time when seasonal work, rural industry and a mobile workforce to complete this work, were all commonplace. The structure and content of this book then, with the central theme of the development and history of the soft-fruit industry in Blairgowrie and its environs, is expanded upon in order to share the memories of some of the people Roger has interviewed during his career about their experiences across a wide spread of rural employments. In chapter 2, we bring together some of these recollections. The selection is eclectic and wide-ranging: from estate work to sugar-beet gathering and salmon fishing to brick kilns. One thing they have in common is that living by the seasons offered only an uncertain way to earn a living, as this extract from Helen Kay, who was born in 1907, illustrates:

> When the fishing finished … they just had to look for a job anywhere. Ma father used to go round the farms an it was always the nearest over to Errol he tried first. And he used to

get a job. Then, of course, when it came on that it was more difficult, the jobs began to get scarce and ma mother used to be quite worried about it, wonderin how she wis going to manage.

In another extract, Bill Nicol, who was born in 1912, recalls the hard physical labour and skill needed for many seasonal employ-ments. Remembering the task of setting up the fly or stake nets at Lunan Bay he said:

This was what we called 'plantin the net'. They had to be in a straight line and you went down at low water. They were planted every four yards; some people put them every three yards.

Until about 1950 we used a tool called the gurl – about six feet high by nine inches diameter. The last few feet being pointed iron. It was best done with six men, three on each side, working the gurl back an forward. The man got a stake over his shoulder ready for planting, while the gurl was put down about three feet into the sand. Each stake was pointed like a pencil and as the men pulled the gurl out quickly the stake was driven in before the sand closed in.

This is a striking image. One can easily imagine those six men working together to try and win the battle with the shifting sodden sands. It must have seemed at times an exasperating endeavour.

Other occupations covered in this chapter include the flax harvest, brick production and estate work. Taken together, the material presented here provides a contextual framework for the chapters which follow.

In chapter 3 we learn more about one of the most significant seasonal jobs: the potato harvest. The potato workers generally came from three societal groups: those who came over from Ireland to work in squads, Scottish Travellers and the local population who lived in the vicinity of the potato fields. This work was physically arduous, not least because the harvest was later in the year when the ground was heavy and the weather unforgiving. The Irish pickers, who came to Scotland in huge numbers, brought with them skill and strength. These skills were prized by the farmers, as this recollection from James McLaren (b.1912) of Dargill demonstrates:

> I always remember the Irishmen. They were really hard workers and could beat us for a day's work because they were used to cutting the peat in Ireland – used to using spades. So they came across here and made light of the work we thought was hard. I mean digging the potatoes by hand.

By contrast, for many casual pickers from the local population, going to the tatties was their first job and could be quite a shock. Here, Mike Henderson, born in 1963, recalled his own experience:

> The work was pretty hard: back-breaking. … My fingers would swell up in the evening, after you'd picked potatoes, because you were bashing these potatoes with the ends of your fingers so the whole finger would swell up. I think it was a reaction to all the cold and the punishment.

Another casual picker, Anne McDonald (b.1946) remarked: 'Oh, the tatties wis murder: it killed yer back … . It wis a holiday. But ye needed a holiday when ye come back'.

In contrast to the tattie work, going to pick the soft-fruit harvest was a much more attractive option. In chapter 4 we come to the main focus of this study, the huge berryfields around Blairgowrie and the experience of those who travelled from near and far to go to the berries.

Many of those who shared their memories with Roger had only fond recollections of their time at the berries. Yet the work was hard and there was little choice about going. The money from the berries provided vital additional income and even small children would be taken along to the berryfields. In a newspaper letter from 1976, (Hodge archive) Mrs Jefferson recalled that in her own case, 'The money earned picking raspberries was a godsend, mother being widowed too early to receive a widow's pension'.

Andrew Hodge, whose grandfather, J. M. Hodge, was pivotal to the expansion of berry growing around Blairgowrie, was one of Roger's interviewees and his testimony helps to set the scene in this chapter. As with the potato work, the berry pickers came from a variety of backgrounds which included local pickers from nearby Dundee as well as those from as far afield as Glasgow and the islands. Ian MacDougall gave Roger one example of a Methil miner who walked through the night to reach the dreels at Blairgowrie by morning. (This was about the time of the '26 strike.) The berry harvest was also a destination for the Scottish Travellers, for whom the annual trip to Blairgowrie was an opportunity to meet up with friends and family.

Partly because of the large number of people required to pick the delicate crop during a harvest season which could run from late June through to September, Andrew recalled that getting pickers was always a challenge. Early on, a large camp at Essendy was established and this provided comfortable accommodation for pickers who came largely from Glasgow and were recruited through the Scottish Council for Women's Trades. As well as the accommodation, other incentives included travel reimbursements and preference was given to families or groups who would commit to stay for the whole season.

Andrew recalled that his father always looked forward to the berry season. It must have been an incredibly lively time. Margaret Miller (1931–2014), whose husband was grieve at the Hodge family farm at Gothens, recalled the pickers who came to them at Gothens:

We must of had at least fifty or sixty [families], maybe more for the Glasgow Fortnight. Some went away after 'the fortnight' if they'd jobs to go back to, you know, men that maybe had jobs. But the majority stayed. ... They'd the time of their life.

... the majority of the Glasgow people stayed till they were finally told that the huts were eventually closing, you know, there was no berries left to pick. But some of them were allowed to stay on for another week. Mr [G. M.] Hodge let them and then he would say, 'Right, the huts are closing such and such a Saturday.'

From a more local perspective, Dundonian Andy Fenwick (b.1964) recalled his own experience of the berries in an extract that reminds us that at the heart of everything was an economic imperative: the berries provided an opportunity to earn money during tough times:

The people that went to the berries, I think, were all one and the same. Nobody viewed themselves as any better than anyone else. We were all there to do the same thing, obviously: pick berries and make some extra money. But you had fun as well. You would hear, in the berryfields, laughter rippling across the fields and people telling jokes and people singing.

For the Scottish Travellers who came to Blairgowrie and made camp by the berry dreels it was also a great opportunity for fun. This recollection comes from Sheila Stewart MBE (1935–2014):

It was a great thing for the people, the non-Travellers and Travellers, to come to Blairgowrie for six weeks of the year. It was a working holiday thing, absolutely brilliant.

... I mean it wasn't just the berry-picking to make money. It was a meeting for the Travellers. Every single year they came and they met. They'd ceilidhs round the fire, and

7

it was unbelievable the fun that went on at the berry-time. It was great …

When the berry industry was at its peak Blairgowrie would be overflowing with people and this could prove challenging for the local law enforcement. Andy McKay was a policeman at Blairgowrie in the 1960s and remembered:

It was perceived as a very challenging place during all the berry season! … You had this seasonal employment, which was largely based [on] people gravitating from Glasgow, Lanarkshire, staying in Blairgowrie for the duration of the berries. And [then] you had overlap situations again with the Dundee holiday period. I should of said that the population would increase quite considerably [and] you could loosely say, all hell was guaranteed to break loose.

In this chapter, we also hear about the infamous 'berry buses' which carried the pickers to and from the berryfields. The transport came in all shapes and sizes and was, evidently, often 'packed to the gunnels' (Jim Devlin) and smelling pretty awful: 'a mixture of berries … and a kind of rotten egg smell' (Andy Fenwick). They were certainly memorable.

One can imagine that, even given all the fun at the berries, Blairgowrie, the farmers, bus drivers, policemen and pickers must have all heaved a sigh of relief at the end of the season. As Andrew Hodge recalled: 'By the end of the season, and perhaps the weather beginning to turn in September, you looked forward to normality being returned … . But it was an enjoyable, busy, happy, noisy time …'.

In 1987, Andrew's father, George M. Hodge, gave a talk on the history of the raspberry industry in Scotland. The script of that talk, printed in full in chapter 5, provides an interesting and useful overview of the industry, with particular regard to the part played by his father, J. M. Hodge, in developing the co-operative venture which would result in Blairgowrie becoming the centre of the soft-fruit industry in Scotland. As George notes, the great success of the Essendy venture was that everyone connected to the small-holdings at Essendy benefitted: 'the company which created them, the smallholders who worked them and the community which gave its labour and goods in exchange for their produce'. The statistics presented here help us to understand how the industry grew and changed over time: 'From a total of 3 or 4 acres in the early 1890s, to tens of acres by the turn of the century, to hundreds of acres when Essendy and Aberuthven came into bearing and, later, to the thousands of acres we have today [1987]'. This paper also highlights the enduring challenges of securing favourable weather and enough pickers: the former to ensure success of the crop and the later to secure the harvest.

In chapter 6 we look more closely at the subject of seasonal dwellings and begin with the accommodation at Essendy and the tin city which was a home-from-home for the pickers.

Roger has been interested in researching seasonal dwellings for most of his collecting career and this chapter includes further oral testimonies relating to other temporary rural living quarters including farm bothies, sweep-net fishing stations and tattie pickers' huts. One recollection, collected from Tom Jarvis Jnr (b.1936) can give a flavour of what to expect:

> I've heard ma wife's father talkin about the Abernethy fishing station in the twenties. Their bothy was on Mugdrum Island and there was no way they could get rid o the rats because Mugdrum Island was infested with rats at that time. He's wakened up in the morning and counted over forty running about the floor of the bothy. It was riddled with holes. You see it was just the earth floor into the bank o the river. They blocked

up one hole and ten minutes later there was another one burrowed through. All their foodstuffs had to be kept in glass jars, and even when they were sitting eating, there was often a rat would jump up on the table to get to the food.

With this account in mind we can turn to the final chapter which collects together recollections of what life was like at home for some of those who, during the season, would have been making the daily journey to the berryfields from Dundee. The noise and stour of the jute mills and recollections of the poor housing help us to understand what day-to-day life was like for many of the berry pickers. Frequent trips to the wash-house, large families crammed into two-bedroom homes and shared outside toilets were all commonplace. Mary Angus (b.1940) recalled of her childhood home: 'I can't remember sitting because there were no seats'. Given this context, the hardship in evidence in earlier chapters can be understood from a slightly different perspective. There are recollections here too about community life and Dundee traditions including the popular pea buster stalls. And we are reminded again of the contribution the berry money made to the family fortunes. Therese Devlin (b.1957) recalls that the berry money allowed her family to get a fridge and get the phone installed, and also buy the school clothes needed for a family of eight. Life was changing though, as the final extract in the book, from Alex Lackie (b.1957) illustrates:

> So we moved to Mid in 1962, an a fev bedroom hoose. Me an ma wee brother played hide an seek for a year. … So, ah o a sudden, eight fowk wae twa bedrooms an an ootside lavvie [went] tae a fev bedroom hoose whaur me an Ricky hed oor ain room, and Peter hed thir ain room, Nancy hed her ain room, mum an dad hed their ain room.

This volume presents us with a picture of life that many of us can hardly imagine enduring. Yet it is a part of our very recent past.

As I write this introduction, uncertainty over the impending Brexit[1] agreement has affected the number of Eastern European pickers coming here to work. In an attempt to redress the balance, farmers are calling for a move away from the term 'economic migrants' to a more representative term, 'guest workers'. Yet again, the industry is faced with the task of securing enough pickers for the harvest and the challenges continue for the soft-fruit growers, just as they did back in the 1890s.

In terms of the amount of collecting Roger has done in his lifetime the present volume is a modest output. Some areas in the book are covered only in passing and there is a generosity here: a call to arms for ethnologists just starting out in their careers. In this I'm reminded of the recent 2018 Bruford lecture[2] at the Scottish Storytelling Centre in Edinburgh. On several occasions the speaker, John Purser, would say as an aside: 'Oh, I've found this reference, but nothing more ... . Maybe someone in the audience will take this forward!' So too with this volume. There is much for the aspiring ethnologist to pick up on here: histories to be gathered from more recent seasonal workers across a range of occupations, not least the berries themselves.

For Roger, this work is a moment in time: a reflection of his career to date, an exploration and sharing of recollections of the berries and other seasonal employments and also a starting-off point for his next project.

* * *

It was anticipated that this book would be 'on the shelves' early April 2020. Then, before the printer could send us the first set of proofs for approval, our world changed – Covid-19 arrived. Within days we became familiar with home isolation, social distancing and eerily quiet roads. In the last days of March 2020, there is already concern within the farming community about how they will be able to find enough workers to pick and process their seasonal crops in the coming months. With the loss of workers from mainland Europe and a virtual lockdown on all but essential travel, this won't be a straightforward issue to resolve. And yet, as we learn in the pages of this book, there was always a problem getting pickers, but they were found and the harvest was gathered. As many non-essential industries and services across the country are now closed for the duration we may yet see as surge in the availability of local pickers. Only time will tell.

Caroline Milligan
2 April 2020

FIELDWORK AND THE ETHNOLOGIST

Chronology

After studying Law at the University of Dundee (1974–78) I went on to the University of Edinburgh as a non-graduating student in the Department of History. I studied settlement, Scottish documents, palaeography, Scottish history and Scottish literature. A favourite subject was the History of Settlement. A pivotal moment came when I was introduced to oral history at a course lecture in 1981 which had been organised by Dr Ian Morrison of the University's geography department. This lecture was about historical traditions on the island of Mull explored using recorded interviews as the source material. The lecturer was a bespectacled scholar called Dr Eric Cregeen[3] of the University's School of Scottish Studies. Eric arrived in what I later came to appreciate was his trademark gabardine raincoat and carrying a cumbersome box that we soon discovered was a reel-to-reel tape recorder. After an introduction he switched the machine on. The class of students fell silent. Everyone was captivated. Lilting grainy-sounding voices from two very old men were describing scenes from a battle fought centuries before their time as if they had been there. This to me was magic. I had never experienced such an original aid to teaching. I forgot that I was in the city and was transported instead back to Mull where I had recently climbed Ben More. For me, that day was an epiphany. Oral history had colour and vibrancy and provided a link with humanity in a way that no other subject had previously achieved for me. I was hooked. I thought to myself, if only I could get hold of a tape recorder the potential would be enormous. I was determined I would travel and reach places by any means possible so that I could play a part in preserving the past for posterity. I recall now that my aspirations at that time were unencumbered by any concerns about my status as a novice field-worker with absolutely no collecting experience.

In pursuit of this goal I acquired the necessary equipment and made some initial fieldwork recordings in Fife. Professor Geoffrey Barrow recommended a move to the School of Scottish Studies so that I could be supported in my fieldwork endeavours and I duly transferred there at the start of 1982. I recall the marvellous ambience of its beautiful departmental library where later I would spend entire summers steeped in the work of earlier folklore collec-tors, both Scottish and Irish. I delved into the School's fantastic sound archive, directed at that time by Hamish Henderson (my specialist supervisor) and Professor John (Jack) MacQueen. One tape I listened to was a recording which Hamish had made of a worthy from Macduff, called Codlins, whose deep bass voice resonated with the Doric. Codlins had been on a sailing schooner. He talked of eating nine fresh herring fillets for breakfast and shared fascinating anecdotes about 'the wonderful boy' (Francie Markis).[4] I envisaged that Hamish had lugged his heavy recording equipment over many miles to seek out this wonderful man before returning to the university, delighted with his endeavours. When I asked him where he had found Codlins, Hamish nonchalantly replied 'Codlins? The university car park. He was one of the atten-dants'. Far from travelling hundreds of miles Hamish had travelled just a few hundred yards across the campus in George Square. I was to reflect on this many times over the subsequent years: as an ethnologist sometimes you need look no further than your own doorstep.

Professor MacQueen, after listening to some of the early recordings that I had made with the Stewart family in Fife, suggested that I concentrate on working with Sandy Stewart, the father of the family group which also included Sandy's wife, Peggie, and their sons, Davie and Sandy. This work was to remain a central focus for me over the next three years and led to the award of a masters degree (M.Litt) in 1985. This study was later written up for *The Book of Sandy Stewart* and published shortly afterwards, in 1988.

Scottish Travellers like the Stewart family have always followed the work and the wider study of seasonal migration has always fascinated me and informed many of the fieldwork choices I have made throughout my career. In 1985–86 I was working as a sound archive supervisor with the Manpower Services Commission (MSC). For 13 months, I worked with unemployed people out of a small office in the Sandeman Library in Perth. Ian MacRae was head librarian there and he was an enthusiastic supporter of our project. Around this time, he put me in touch with some salmon fishers on the Tay and, after the end of the MSC project, I followed up this connection, making a number of recordings with the Tay fishermen especially over one long weekend in 1987.

Sadly, I undertook very little fieldwork recording for much of the 1990s. Welcome exceptions included a memorable time in 1991 where, during a week-long stay at Whitehills on the Moray Firth coast, I collected folk-life memories of the women who had gone to work as gutting quines, following the migrating shoals of herring from Orkney to Yarmouth. One often relies on a local person to introduce you to a new area and George Gray, a former head librarian of the University of St Andrews, who stayed in Whitehills, was kind enough to put wheels in motion for me on this occasion.

I went back into university in the late 1990s and graduated from Dundee in 1999 with a PhD titled, 'Seasonal Workers: Their

Dwellings and Living Conditions in Scotland, 1770–1970'. Material from this study forms a small amount of the research included here.[5]

Methodology

Early fieldwork collectors in Ireland were encouraged to keep journals which chronicled their experiences, including providing detailed accounts of the recording process and impressions of the storytellers they encountered. I sought to emulate this practice on a cycling odyssey that took me coast to coast across Scotland and over to the Uists and Benbecula in September 1984.[6] Here I carried out my fieldwork by taking down verbatim what I was told, in English, in conversations with informants. I found that travelling by bicycle helped to establish a rapport in that people appreciated that I had made an effort to reach them, quite often in extremely poor weather. One experience keenly etched in my memory is of arriving, drenched, in Liniclate, South Uist. Here Jane Gillies (b.1900), originally from Earsary on Barra, produced her own small mono-cassette recorder with which we recorded local Barra traditions and her memories of the herring gutting at Yarmouth.

In Uist and Eriskay I largely wrote material in longhand before reading the script back to my informants. If they were satisfied with the veracity, then I would ask them to sign their name at the end. It could be a painstakingly slow way to collect yet I found it practical for collecting shorter anecdotal stories, information about local history and derivations of place-names from oral tradition. Moreover, there was a chance to assess the efficacy of collecting in English in a Gaelic-speaking heartland such as the Uists. I found in some cases oral history informants were less intimidated (if the word is not too strong) by my notebook and pen than they would have been by a recording machine. Where Gaelic was the first language there was a chance to concentrate on shorter items. I found that reading back what I had written down verbatim seemed to go down well. This is perhaps not too surprising, given that we are generally reluctant to hear the sound of our own recorded voice for the first time.

The etiquette of collecting in Highland areas was referred to by Donald MacDonald of Eriskay when I encountered this now, sadly, largely forgotten figure in the world of folklore on a trip there in 2001. Donald told me that the people 'preferred you to come in the evening because they were always out at the land' during the daylight hours.

An earlier opportunity to collect closer to home came through my friends Angus Morrison and Steve Turnbull and the bothies they had stayed in as young men while doing seasonal work on the River Tay. This connection re-ignited my interest in seasonal work and migration and provided the focus for much of my later research and, subsequently, this book. Many of the bothies were falling into desuetude and so, in February 1988, I set out to photograph or sketch them, to interview the men who slept in them and generally record all I could about that way of life and its associated material culture. I much preferred to learn by being out in the real world. Gathering empirical fieldwork and being on the road were also strong motivators. At one point, off Usan on the Angus coast, I took the opportunity from salmon fisherman Dave Pullar to go out in his sea coble and photograph him and his son fishing the bag nets for wild salmon.[7] Experiences like this were not, for me, everyday occurrences and these encounters fired my passion for oral history collecting. They continue to remain vivid and inspirational to this day.

With the more recent fieldwork research included in this book I found myself working much closer to home. I was searching for material relating to both the berry and tattie picking and, mindful of Codlins, the university car park attendant, I began by asking friends and neighbours. This was a new experience for me. I was now working in Dundee, a city which is home to 142,000 people. On the face of it there is more anonymity here than in a small rural community, but cities are often a collection of linked communities and very often retain a strong sense of community at a local level: this was certainly true in Dundee. I had a couple of vibrant recruiting grounds. One was a charity shop, the other a bookshop and both gave me a surprisingly good number of enthusiastic informants. It proved a fruitful and hugely enjoyable way of working. I had to think on my feet. Through the initial contact with friends, neighbours and key contacts my range of city informants soon expanded to match my earlier experiences recording in rural situations. Interview locations extended out to encompass a wide array of settings which included the eyrie of a castle, a tenement kitchen and one interview conducted with passengers while we travelled together in a white transit van. For interviews where a face-to-face opportunity was impractical, I made telephone interviews. The range of interviewees, in both age and occupation, was incredibly diverse and included: a bank manager, boat-builder and joiner, booksellers, brickies, business-men, butcher, a carer, a civil servant, engineers, farmworkers and fishermen, a graphic designer, handy-man, landscape gardener, musicians, a nurse, policemen, printers, a roofer and roughcaster, a solicitor, students, a supermarket employee, Travellers and war veterans.[8] This diversity, in location and type of contributor, was both challenging and rewarding.

On each occasion, the oral history interview is a dynamic, ever-changing experience – this is a huge part of the enjoyment of such work. There are as many different types of interviewee as there are interviews and one can never foretell how valuable individual contributors will be to one's research. During my fieldwork I came into contact with some veritable comedians and complete extroverts. Some contributors will appreciate the worth of what they can tell you, recognising perhaps that the world is changing so fast it is almost an imperative to commit their memories to the collective record. Others will simply enjoy reminiscing about the past, reflecting perhaps on a time when they were more a part of society than they might feel at the present time. Still others will be surprised to find their memories are considered valuable at all. One person might be a born communicator whose recollections are naturally rich in detail. Another might be far less forthcoming and provide only essential facts, either due to their natural demeanour, a sense that their contribution is of little value, or shyness about the interview process. And, of course, interviews will vary in length considerably. Sometimes one short interview will suffice while at other times multiple interview sessions with the same person will be more appropriate and might still prove insufficient. What we can say with confidence is that every interviewee will bring something new to what we can know about our shared history. It is the job of the interviewer to reassure and encourage each interviewee in order to facilitate the best possible interview for the interviewee.

An essential skill for any oral history collector is the ability to listen carefully and this is a skill that develops only with practice. Often, while carrying out an interview, the collector will recognise the moment they hear something special or unique and will make a mental note to follow that up. As they develop their skill they will be able to recognise when the interviewee has more to tell. In my own experience, I have frequently interviewed individual contributors over multiple sessions. For this study, I recall interviewing one person three times over the course of ten years and each occasion yielded yet more new information and insights.

When working on the research for this book it seemed at times that every person of a certain age that I spoke with in Dundee had been to the berry picking or the potato harvest. As a result, I was taking my recorder with me everywhere so that I could carry out interviews when the opportunity arose. I was continually struck by the openness of the interviewees and by the affection and humour with which they recalled their time at the berries or the tatties. Despite the hard work, there was a lot of fun to be had, especially at the berries when those summer weeks made a change to the normal day-to-day lives back home: even if the primary reason was usually to earn vital money to cover essentials, such as buying school clothes. Although the memories were largely happy ones, quite often interviewees would be recounting quite personal details and I felt privileged and humbled that they would share their memories with me. As a result of our time together contributors have gained my sincere respect and some have become good friends. People have often gone out of their way to help me with no expectation of reward and I am indebted to them all.

While it is valuable to collect oral testimonies it is also the priority and responsibility of the oral history collector to ensure that this material is then made available to a wider public and to do this with integrity and balance. The rich detail provided by those who have contributed over the years adds greatly to the historical record by providing first person, nuanced accounts which enrich our understanding of our shared cultural history. I have been delighted to contribute to the dialogue which has seen, in recent years, oral history and the spoken word gain a validity that has hitherto been denied this form of record. I feel that the spoken word and personal memory now sit comfortably alongside their written counterparts: diaries, letters or memoirs. Gathering information from as diverse a research group as we can enables us to see patterns across a common theme and also, so importantly, allows us to get nearer to the depth of detail which is needed if we are to try to capture a true representation of the lived experience for any given time and place.

Equipment

The equipment used by collectors has changed considerably since mechanical recording began. Factors such as the size, weight, number of parts and the available recording time for any given device have been subject to near continuous change and this inevitably plays a part in the interview dynamic. My own collecting experience has now spanned several decades but we can look even further back to see how equipment has changed over time and reflect on how this change may have influenced what is collected.

Early collectors often used the Ediphone, a machine that weighed a hefty fifty pounds. The interviewees spoke into a large voice box and the recordings were etched onto wax cylinders. One imagines that the arrival of the collectors, with this (or similar) equipment, must have made quite an impact. In 1996, I corresponded with Professor Derick S. Thomson[9] on the subject of collecting. He told me:

> I was involved in recording the like of Duncan MacDonald, at
> Easter 1949, along with Calum Maclean.[10] This was during a
> visit made to South Uist along with Professor Angus McIntosh
> (Professor of English Language) and David Abercrombie (Head
> of the Department of Linguistics). Like them, I was on the staff
> of Edinburgh University that year (as an assistant), and both
> McIntosh and Abercrombie were among those whose plans
> finally resulted in the founding of the School of Scottish
> Studies in 1951 … . It was a Ferrograph,[11] I think that we used,
> or possibly a still earlier model, and the power came from the
> car/van parked outside the house. I seem to remember that a
> squawking hen caused some recording problems indoors.

By 1962 collectors from the School of Scottish Studies had access to more readily portable recording machines but still relied on the older Vortexion tape machines when they wanted to ensure that they made the best recording possible. I heard this next anecdotal passage from Donald Archie MacDonald[12] when we sat in his car outside the family home in North Uist. I remember it was well after midnight before we concluded the taped interview:

> I was very concerned with making good fieldwork recordings
> at that stage, and instead of taking one of the smaller battery
> portables, such as I'd used in 1954, we took out the full-sized
> Vortexion, which as you know weighed as much as a sack of
> coal and was, I suppose, two and a half feet by two feet. Ian
> Crawford and I carried that in sacks on our back out to
> Hacklett (Benbecula) over the moorland in the dark, using
> torches. ... But that wasn't an everyday experience. There's
> also things like that remarkable man, Peter Morrison,[13] at
> Sandbank in Grimsay [North Uist] ... well, Sandbank at that
> stage became an island at high tide. There was a road into it
> and you took the car out across the sands and stayed at the
> house until the tide went down again.

Balancing quality of the recording with practicality, both in terms of transportability and how appropriate the machine might be in a particular interview situation, is always a consideration for the oral history fieldworker. Fortunately, as the years have passed, machines have become smaller and easier to travel with, while still ensuring good quality recordings. In the early 1980s my own field-work equipment was a Marantz Superscope C-205 cassette machine. I recall that, at £99, it was three times the price I had only recently paid for my old Austin van. To protect the recorder from the elements I used a wax-proofed angler's game bag which the machine slotted neatly inside. The front pockets were ideal for notebook and tapes and, later, were especially appropriate for the 5-inch reels I used when collecting with the portable Uher tape machine. The Marantz Superscope proved ideal for my needs – and robust enough for the road – while the lack of extra cabling made it more practical in many situations, such as around the Travellers' camp when I was working with Sandy Stewart and his family. The Superscope had a useful index counter (helpful for navigating recordings), variable speed control (essential for slowing down rapid speech) and a trusty pause button that stood up to a lot of wear. I found it an ideal workhorse.

Subsequently, for better, more professional recordings I used the Uher 4000 Report Monitor. At a speed of 3¾ inches per second it gave good quality recordings. This was the machine used by broadcasters, explorers, scientists and folklorists in all parts of the world, very often in less than ideal conditions. To power the machine, I used a dry cell battery which could be re-charged and the equipment was always pre-checked by Fred Kent, the highly competent head technician at the School of Scottish Studies. Although I often used an omni-directional mic, I found a superior directional mic was better for short interview pieces and indeed also for longer recordings with a single contributor.

For total ease of carrying, I started using a recording Sony Walkman in 1986. This came with an external lapel-clasp mic which was on a rather short lead but it did the business and there was no real mystery about its use. I continued to use this cassette machine for over twenty-five years until the pause button ceased to function. Better still is the machine I presently use for sound-bites, longer interviews and telephone recordings. This is a Sony Voice Recorder and uses cassette tapes which I can thankfully still buy at my local supermarket. It is not much larger than a packet of cigarettes and I have found it ideal for adaptation to various scenarios, although it is only really suitable as an audio notebook and not appropriate for making high quality sound recordings.

Of course, the choice of equipment is, to a large extent, dictated by the available technology. In speaking about photography, Gus Wylie noted, 'There is probably more nonsense spoken about the mystiques and techniques of photographs than anything else', and he warns of being over-zealous about the mechanics of his trade. This is certainly true also in the context of fieldwork and recording devices. If the fieldworker is to fulfil their role as facilitator, enabling their informant to tell their story in their own way, it is vital the collector feels confident and comfortable with their chosen recording device. Achieving this will leave them free to concentrate on their interviewee and on listening to what is being said so that they can then ask appropriate follow-up questions.

The latest digital recording devices are discreet and capable of recording for several hours at a time. This has the great advantage of freeing up the fieldworker to concentrate on the content of the interview but comes with additional ethical and practical considerations. The recording machine can be so small that it can be forgotten by the interviewee so the collector has to monitor their role as facilitator carefully to avoid unwittingly allowing their interviewee to say more than they are comfortable with. Oral history interviewing can be a wonderful experience for both the collector and the contributor but it is also very often mentally and physically exhausting. Although it is still my practice to record on C90 cassettes (45 minutes recording time per side) for the vast majority of collectors it is no longer necessary to change reels or cassettes every 16, 32, or 45 minutes and so the collector also has to be sensitive to recognising when their contributor needs a break.

I would certainly urge any aspiring fieldworker to just get out and get started. In a trite way, doing basic fieldwork is just common sense. However, I believe that to be a good ethnologist, you must keep your interviewee at the centre of your consideration at all times and develop your craft with practice and reflection.

Fieldwork

In the third week of January 1982, several months after my encounter with Eric Cregeen and the old lads from Mull, I decided to set off on foot into Galloway. I began my journey in style with my friend, Brendan Coleman, giving me a lift in his Alfa Romeo down to Lockerbie. I remember it was torrential rain all the way and as I watched the tail lights of vehicles on the A74 morph into a watercolour red I pondered on the wisdom of such a fieldtrip, my first ever at this time of the year and also my first adventure outside Fife.

Next morning it was night into day. Sunshine bounced off the whitewashed farm buildings of the Dumfriesshire countryside. My morale was raised and the rain of the previous night forgotten. A bus took me out to New Abbey. The mill was closed, the pubs shut, Sweetheart Abbey not yet open. I walked out that midwinter morning and made my way along by the Solway Firth. I had come prepared to walk and hitchhike and my luck was in when a family in a bullnose Morris stopped and squeezed me into the back of their car. Thankful for the kindness of strangers I got round by Kippford, Dalbeattie and into Kirkcudbright. Here I recorded a retired fisherman who was in a sheltered housing flat. I had just come off the street, explained what I was doing and why, and the warden immediately put me into the company of John Pollard, aged 71.

Later that year I travelled the length and breadth of Scotland: from Crail in Fife to Cuidrach on Skye and from Crocketford in Galloway to Durness in the far north-west of Sutherland. On memorable fieldtrips as I hitchhiked, walked, cycled, and travelled by rail and sea, intuition and serendipity played their part in the success of my endeavours. My own travels pale into insignificance compared to the American folksong collector and blues specialist Alan Lomax (1915–2002) who, in the 1930s with his father, John, clocked up 16,000 miles travelling throughout the USA in just four months.[14] Nonetheless, my own travels during the 1980s proved to be a personal odyssey. I found being able to spend extended periods of time out in the field extremely worthwhile and valued.

Other people in other occupations came into the scope of field-work that year: retired farmers and farmworkers, Travellers, wood contractors, crofters, shepherds, housewives, a visual artist, a pearl-fisher, a schoolmistress in Wester Ross, a docker's widow from Methil, miners, a joiner and an undertaker. Each encounter inspired me as I developed as a fieldworker, gathering interviews which I would find myself re-visiting and re-exploring many times over the subsequent years.

I was grateful to another helpful friend, Bill Reid, for providing vital assistance on many of my fieldwork trips. Bill was a sales representative for a building firm and visited outlying farms in his blue Ford Capri (complete with snow chains in the boot) and he often got me to hubs for buses and trains. Some of the best field-trips were organised through contact men such as Kenny Horne, a gamekeeper on the Atholl estate in Perthshire or Jimmy Henderson, a former reporter with the *Daily Express* and also, at that time, editor of *The Northern Times* in Golspie.[15] Jimmy put an office and phone at my disposal; definitely going the extra mile to help me. Through Jimmy I contacted Simon MacLeod, the local butcher for Lochinver, who supplied me with names of infor-mants for Assynt. My trip there, in the spring of 1983, was funded by the School of Scottish Studies and part of my time was spent collecting material relating to place-names for the School's Place-Name Survey. On that trip, to cut down on the weight of material that I had to carry, I would periodically send the annotated maps and completed notebooks back to Edinburgh, to the ever method-ical and efficient Ian Fraser who was working with the survey at that time.

Often I would travel with my recording gear and camera and virtually nothing else except the clothes on my back. I definitely had a wanderlust and was delighted that I could fruitfully combine travelling and collecting. Getting around the country by public transport in those days was an adventure in itself and postbuses often came into their own when trying to reach more remote areas of the country. On one occasion I remember I took the postbus out of Drumbeg in Assynt before picking up another, a minibus this time, which took me to Durness near the very north-west corner of the Scottish mainland. At Durness I recorded the remarkable George MacKenzie who had over 41 years service with the Northern Lighthouse Board, part of that time as a principal lighthouse keeper serving on wild rock stations in the Atlantic. He excelled in relating tales of his adventures and I have always felt extremely fortunate that our paths crossed.[16]

At other times, the life of a wandering ethnologist was not such an easy life. On leaving Strath Oykel one spring morning in 1982 my interviewee, pearlfisher Eddie Davies, and I went our separate ways. He had set me down at a road junction and my outstretched thumb was seen by a gentleman who stopped in his Range Rover, picked me up and then dropped me off, at the former drovers' inn at Inchnadamph miles from nowhere. No bus appeared. As the heavens opened, thunder rumbled and in a force nine gale I had no option but to trudge the remaining nine miles west, into Lochinver.

Interviewees

I had an early interest in roads and charters and planned, at the outset of my fieldwork career, to speak to Scottish Travellers to ask them about the old roads. It was with this in mind that, in the winter of 1981, I decided to record a Travelling family who were living in a gelly[17] outside the Fife village of Upper Largo. I remember my first visit with great affection. We were in the depths of an Arctic winter and snow lay thick on the ground when I first called on the Stewart family. My hosts welcomed me into their tent and as I ducked under the door flap it was to find myself entering an almost medieval world. The family had no electricity and a stick fire in an old bread tin set on two bricks provided their only source of heat. Water was collected from a gushing spout half a mile away. That evening the tent rocked with storytelling and laughter as they shared their world with me. I had a Dixon's ghetto blaster tape machine with me and also a copy of Dick Gaughan's seminal album, *Handful of Earth*. I put the music on and as we listened we drank a little more wine and some beer. I can well imagine that never before or since did the Archie Fisher ballad, *The Snows They Melt The Soonest* receive such an appreciative audience as on that night. Never did it seem more appropriate as the winter sun dipped low and the icy realisation of camping out in sub-zero temperatures hit home.[18]

Some weeks later, one Saturday night in Dumfriesshire, I landed up in a motel by the side of the busy Stranraer to Dumfries road with much to reflect on. Fieldwork can, at times, be a lonely pursuit but this never put me off and to shorten the road there was usually someone to strike up a conversation with. A man I spoke to in the bar that night spurred me to pick up the phone and contact a local farmer who was described to me as a 'bit of a wag, a worthy'. This was Wull Halliday of Meikle Kirkland, which was a short distance off the old military road near Crocketford. Over the telephone that evening Wull gave me directions to his farm and the next morning found me out in the mist, clambering over drystone dykes to reach his back door. Wull came out to meet me in boots, a bonnet, dungarees and, over them, a tweed jacket. He was one of the most natural Galloway speakers and had that knack of putting you right at ease in his company. Violet, Wull's wife, had lit the coal fire and produced a marvellous spread for my visit. As the tape rolled, Wull told me that it was his aunt, Sarah, who had passed the family stories on to him. Her father had been 'born on the nicht o Waterloo', Wull recalled. There was thus an unbroken passage of almost 170 years in family tradition and I felt privileged that he shared his time and history with me. All expectations I might have had of his contribution were surpassed. As well as humorous anecdotes he also told me about horse-trading gypsies from Kendal and of the time of the General Strike, 1926, when the Kirkland barn provided a home for many unemployed miners. Over the years other overnight visitors to the barn had included hobos, men of the road and the rails, some of whom were veterans of the First World War. They were all given refuge by Wull Halliday and his family. I left Wull feeling buoyed by our encounter. I found him and his way of life enriching and truly special. Friendships forged in this way are a bonus to the vocation of the ethnological fieldworker. Although I would not meet him again, I still keep in touch with his family. His memory lives on.

Other notable encounters spring to mind. In South Uist, until his death in 1954, lived the great Gaelic storyteller, Duncan Mac-Donald of Peninerine. Donald Archie MacDonald of the School of Scottish Studies has described the repertoire of hero tales held by Duncan MacDonald as being from 'undoubtedly the greatest classicist of his age who possessed a spectacular memory that allowed word for word rendition of the longer tales'.[19] I caught up with Duncan's son, Donald John, in September of 1984. He too was a bard and had collected family tradition, in manuscript, for the School. I cycled the twenty-mile round trip to visit him. It was a joy, on a calm day, to travel along these quiet single-track roads. The muffled boom of the surf pounding over the machair[20] was like a message from another world. Here at Peninerine the next stop west is St Kilda and, beyond that, North America.

Returning to Assynt in 1983, at the behest of Geordie Mathieson, a garrulous eccentric who had been in the Merchant Navy, I helped

29

move a sideboard in the back of his white Morris pick-up. Petrol was in an empty Bell's whisky bottle, the door handles were fashioned from orange binder twines and there were no brakes save for the handbrake. Untaxed and with the existence of an MOT as likely as selling mince rolls to Martians, we descended down the steep Stoer brae. 'Ach, hold tight,' Geordie quipped. 'I'll use the clutch and pud her into reverse'. No big deal. After holding on for grim death it was mission accomplished and I started recording Geordie near the witching hour. The half bottle of Grouse we shared that night helped him rattle through a fraction of his hilarious repertoire. Then I heard birdsong. Before I knew it, the dawn was breaking through. I staggered back to my digs, exhausted. On that occasion I had used the portable Uher which took five-inch reels and we got through two or three of these that night.[21]

Amongst others I tracked down was a clergyman of 99 years and eleven months. This was the Revd William Milne, who was, at that time, 'the Faither o the Kirk'.[22] He lived with his housekeeper in Crail. I was allotted only 15 minutes with him as he was very frail. During our brief time together, he told me about when he had the offer to play professional football with Glasgow Rangers and of being capped several times for the Scotland rugby XV.

On the shores of the Solway Firth I recall riding over the hard packed sand in Sandy Munro's American Jeep to assist the salmon netsmen clean seaweed and other detritus from their stake nets. The catch was poor: one grilse and sea trout. Back in the bothy a bottle was passed round, stories told and laughter ensued: the trials of the day were then quickly forgotten, but Sandy and that experience remain vivid in my mind to this day.

Pivotal work on salmon netsmen, which is referred to in this study, was carried out back in 1987 and included in my PhD thesis. With me on that occasion was Annette Ratcliff. At that time everything worked by word of mouth and in one weekend, as a result of a number of interviews in both Abernethy and Newburgh, I was able to record material which reflected a wide variety of experiences from both salmon netsmen and members of their families.

When I visited Whitehills, on the Banffshire coast, in 1991, the population was about 960 with nine whitefish boats in its harbour. The main employer was Downie's fish processing plant. My oldest informant was a charming, modest lady called Miss Isa Ritchie (b.1886). I worked using a notebook and pen as she told me about her own travels and endurance: gutting was not for the faint-hearted. Others I met in Whitehills included Mary Bella Findlay, Belle Thomson and landlady, Lena Brown. They were the salt of the earth. Next stop was the Broch[23] where I shared digs with a squad of builders who, as I recall, ate gigantic fry-ups every morning. At the local public library in Fraserburgh, Loraine Noble put me in touch with her aunt, Mrs Jessie Watt (*née* MacLeod) (b.1904). Over afternoon tea in the company of this warm-natured lady I made notes on aspects of the migratory gutting life recalled from her sharply attuned memory. Jessie and Loraine were rare gems of a kind I did not meet every day.

For the present study I was often making recordings in a local charity shop and this presented another set of challenges. It was important not to disrupt the normal day-to-day activity of the shop and as a result interviews were often short – ten to 15 minutes being a typical session. The recordings were made with a small, hand-held recorder. For these interviews I chose not to record introductions as I found doing so made the encounter too formal which could have a negative influence on the subsequent discussion. By dint of the venue, the interviewees in the charity shop were mostly women. Some were extroverts who would encourage others to take part and I enjoyed the part that they played in my research endeavours. In other situations, rapport was built-up gradually with those contributors who were naturally more reticent or reserved. However, persistence was always rewarded and some of my best contributors have been those who were initially less sure about being interviewed.

Other fieldworkers

As well as learning my craft through the activity of being an ethnologist I was also guided by those who had gone before me through both personal contact and published writings.

In South Uist, Donald John MacDonald had told me how the early collectors used to beat a path to his father's door. One such visitor was Donald MacDonald of Eriskay, who had been a student at the University of Glasgow and was at the forefront of collecting stories from Duncan of Peninerine while he was employed as a collector with the Irish Folklore Commission (IFC). An Comunn Gaidhealach, in Inverness, became aware of this and supplied MacDonald with a Dictaphone, an innovation which was relatively new in the 1930s. After transcribing, the completed wax cylinders used with the Dictaphone were sent from Eriskay to Inverness to be 'shaved' and recycled. Although this process meant a lot of original oral material was lost, the Dictaphone did mark a significant development in ethnological fieldwork recording. Dr J. L. Campbell of Canna excelled with older technology. Another was K. C. Craig[24] who noted Duncan's stories in longhand, sometimes over successive nights, and Donald John told me he saw that Craig contracted writer's cramp from these endeavours.

Collecting in those days called for stamina, not just for the strength to carry the heavy recording machines. Ferries from Eriskay were sailboats and, even into the 1960s, it could take as long as 24 or 36 hours to reach the far north or the Hebrides from Edinburgh. Many Highland roads were single track, ferries were slower, bridges and causeways not yet built and one could easily become stormbound and stranded. In my own time I recall one arduous ten-hour sea voyage from Oban to Castlebay, Barra, which was followed, thankfully, by a much easier 18-minute flight from Barra's cockleshell beach to Benbecula. Quite a journey and, in 1980, I recall that the cost was £15.10 in total, which included the plane fare of £7.

Donald MacDonald of Eriskay explained that his entrée into collecting came while he was a student at the University of Glasgow in the 1930s:

> I met Professor Delargy (of the Irish Folklore Commission) through a friend of mine in Barra. The friend suggested that he should set me to start collecting for him. He wrote to me and I was employed by the IFC [and paid] enough to cover my expenses. It was mostly the Eriskay collection, about 400 typed pages …
>
> Professor Delargy collected mostly in the Aran islands, Galway and Connemara. He really had to rough it and would tell me that he would find himself covered in lice in the morning, you know, with having the cattle in the houses.[25]

Professor James H. 'Seamus' Delargy was an incredibly power-ful driving force behind the collection and dissemination of oral traditions in Ireland. *The Gaelic Story-Teller with some Notes on Gaelic Folk Tales*,[26] his evocation of the world of the Gaelic story-teller, is a short classic of its genre.[27] In it he captures a sense of place and a sense of time and also a sense of being in the right place at the right time. During one summer afternoon in Edinburgh I recall the impact this had on me as I sat and studied it in the back room of the School of Scottish Studies library with the sunlight dappling the pages that I turned so eagerly. Here were stories of the old type, told by fishermen, quarriers and men of the road and learning this was to inform and influence my future fieldwork endeavours. Professor Delargy had started his fieldwork in the 1920s. Inside a cabin near the windswept coast of Kerry he sat on a bag of salt (used for curing fish) while he wrote at a table, word for word, what his friend, the tradition bearer Seán Ó Conaill, narrated to him. Each day, before they started their work, Delargy would have helped with household chores; in this way it was a two-way exchange, a sharing. Library work on these hot summer days would suspend thoughts of fieldwork in my mind like the motes that danced between the window and the bookshelves. Such days meant that I enthused all the more at the thought of leaving the city for the islands or some distant place apart on the mainland.

For the student of ethnology a book that captures the background, problems and intellectual excitement of collecting folklore in a rural setting is Michael J. Murphy's *Tyrone Folk Quest*.[28] His advice is sound when he writes that the dedicated collector 'should avoid publicity like a man on the run: should work like a poteen-maker in his den' and adroitly win over the confidence of his desired contributors. Based on two handwritten journals completed in the period 1949–52 in County Tyrone, this book provides a true flavour of collecting oral tradition and should be read in conjunction with Donald Archie MacDonald's guide on the same subject[29] by anyone keen to develop their practice.

As I have developed as an ethnologist a number of my own contemporaries have also provided inspiration and guidance. Ian MacDougall has done a great deal for oral history through his extensive collecting and subsequent publications.[30] Along with ethnologist and poet, Angus Martin,[31] Ian has investigated corners of our past that have often been overlooked or forgotten. So, too, have broadcasters Jimmie Macgregor[32] and Billy Kay,[33] the latter with his ground-breaking *Odyssey* radio programmes. Professor Sandy Fenton inspired me with his studies on regional ethnology and aspects of material culture. My own development as a field-worker was supported and enhanced by knowing Sandy Ives who wrote a marvellous book about woodsman and song-maker, Joe Scott. Sandy, along with his wife, Bobby, visited me at my home in Perthshire, from Maine in the USA, in May 1987. He was one of the most modest academics I have ever met. This modesty belied a dynamic passion for folk-life research that fired my own enthusiasm: it was infectious. His book, *The Tape-Recorded Interview*, is a manual that still delivers on relevant sections such as interview techniques and it has an excellent index and bibliography.[34] At the School of Scottish Studies, Hamish Henderson, Donald Archie MacDonald, Jack MacQueen, Alan Bruford, Eric Cregeen and Ian Fraser were inspirational mentors. They were active at a time when it was possible to devote more time to fieldwork than was subsequently possible and they have left us a fine legacy of source material and scholarly endeavours.

At the end of the day, recording and representing the rich history of our cultural past is a communal effort and everyone working in our field makes a contribution and can provide inspiration and guidance for aspiring collectors and seasoned practitioners alike.

Reflection

I found fieldwork invigorating, exhilarating and tiring. It found me free from time-watching, free from care and free from convention. I was passionate about recording and about the role I could play in giving people a voice and, through that, contribute towards the creation of a meaningful and detailed record of our shared experience.

As a fieldworker, no two days were the same. In my time I have dossed down on the pearlfisher's sofa, had a piece with backwoodsman Willie Birrell in his tarred felt hut on the braes of Tulliemet, enjoyed homemade soup and draught Belhaven Best with Syd and Margaret Scroggie at their cottage in Strathmartine, cycled in thick haar through the Carse of Gowrie, watched a coal puffer steam out of Castlebay, taken a midnight dram on the ferry leaving Lewis and been woken at dawn by the cold hand of snow as Bob Russell and I bivvied on concrete in the shell of a shepherd's bothy on the isle of Eigg. These encounters added colour and excitement to my life experience and, plucked out of the air at random, are just a few of my cherished memories. Oral history collecting is a very human endeavour and nearly always a pleasurable one but it is also a very necessary endeavour if we are to seek to ensure that our shared history is democratic, with wide representation of people and experience across all strata of society.

Right at the very end of the collecting period for this book I completed some short interviews with three third-year art students. They provided useful personal input on their own early life experience as well as reflecting on other aspects of life in twenty-first-century Scotland. These interviews provided the worthwhile contribution of youthful experience and memory and may lead to further work. Other projects for the future include the life story of a lady in the north-west Highlands who I recorded numerous times over the course of one year, as well as recollections of engineers and draughtsmen from local heavy industry operations which have now declined. Over a period of twenty months I also collected the oral memoir of an Antarctic whaler who was a former deck mess-boy. He was terminally ill and attended a Marie Curie hospice in Edinburgh. Whaling is a subject that rankles but the dangerous lives and living conditions of the men on whale-catchers and factory ships have tended to be overlooked and should be added to the record. Like a lot of field research, uncomfortable truths are sometimes found and need to be documented: lest we forget. And so the work of the ethnologist carries on.

The Book

The outline for this book was drafted with Mark Mulhern. Primarily an oral history of the people who went to the 'berries' this study also includes fieldwork gathered over a number of decades relating to this and other outdoor seasonal occupations, both agricultural and industrial, most notably the potato harvest and Tay salmon fishing. Perthshire, Angus and parts of Fife provide the geographical focus. This is an area where I have carried out extensive fieldwork and one that has a long history of seasonal work due to its abundant agricultural landscape. It is hoped that this study will be of value as a comparative example for researchers working on similar studies in other geographical areas. A springboard for this current study has been the ground-breaking studies completed by T. M. Devine[35] and, more recently, Heather Holmes.[36] A good deal of attention has been given to the grain harvest[37] and the nineteenth century and this book seeks to provide material to contribute towards a complementary consideration of other land-based industries in the twentieth century. Also of inspired interest was the wide swathe of society represented in *Scottish Voices* by T. C. Smout and Sydney Wood.[38]

The material presented here is intended to give the reader an understanding of the rural scene at a time when the agricultural landscape supported a far larger workforce than it does today. As well as the core chapters on rural working practices, interview material relating to the domestic milieu during this period is included to illustrate the day-to-day life of those who, outwith the berry or tattie weeks, spent most of the year settled in an urban environment.

When it came to gathering testimonies from the people closely associated with the berryfields of Blair, Andrew Hodge, solicitor and grandson of Mr J. M. Hodge, has been a tremendous supporter. He gave me the use of the boardroom in his legal firm's Blairgowrie offices and also organised a number of people for me to interview. I saw them individually: a former baillie, a driver, a grower, a grieve's widow, and a retired ironmonger – the last from Alyth. The informants soon forgot about the formality of the surroundings and recording equipment as they reminisced about their life experience and the berry times at Blair.

To gain a feel for the subject of seasonal work I undertook a literary tramp of old newspapers in the Central Library, Dundee. These included back copies of *The Courier & Advertiser* and *People's Journal*. Combined with the meticulous scrapbook cuttings of J. M. Hodge, these enabled me to define areas of study and frame research questions. By August 2011, one month into the current project, I had already recorded 17 different interviews. A number of themes came up again and again, including the ubiquitous berry buses which ferried the pickers to and from the berries. Pickers, drivers and even retired policemen all told me something different about their own berry bus experiences. Others provided more particular details, sometimes relating to life in the urban communities. One of the oldest contributors was Miss Helen Jackson, who died just a fortnight short of her 100th birthday. She told me about her early visits to the cinema when the arrival of the talkies caused a sensation.

The interviewees whose voices appear in the following pages were all local to the area of enquiry. However, it is important to remember that other groups, such as the Glasgow pickers or those from Eastern Europe, have also played their part in the wider history of the Tayside berryfields. While there are no interviews with pickers who came up from Glasgow, the importance of their contribution to the berry industry can be imagined through historical information provided for the camp at Essendy and presented here. Similarly, the Irish pickers whose contribution to the potato industry is widely acknowledged are represented here by those who encountered them and recalled their own memories of this important workforce. The topical subject of East European migrant workers coming to pick the soft fruit crop was something I tried to explore through a short questionnaire to two men from the Czech Republic. Their cousin acted as scribe and translator.

The language barrier and employment fears meant answers were very short and limited to comments on the basic necessities. That said, budget air flights, the Scottish weather and accommodation in static caravans all merited mention. I hope their story will be told by other fieldworkers in the future.

The process of transcribing interview material is always time-consuming and, given my practice of completing transcriptions as soon as possible after the recording session, this often meant working through the night was the only option. The transcribed interviews which form the research material for the present study filled nearly twelve A4 notebooks, each of 160 pages. The intense method adopted for transcribing the interviews was exhausting but also incredibly helpful when engaging with, and then trying to hold on to, the large quantities of textual material.

Speech in the interviews covered a variety of dialects and every effort has been made to ensure each transcription is as faithful as possible to the voice and intonation of the interviewee so that the reader can hear the contributor speak with an authentic voice. I was aided in this endeavour by the *Concise Scots Dictionary* and *Scottish National Dictionary* (*SND*). Norman Watson's *The Dundee Dicshunury*[39] brought out the fuller flavour of expression in a readable way while the *Penguin English Dictionary* proved to have masterly coverage of the contemporary lexicon. I used this last dictionary more than any other until it fell apart and was replaced by a pocket *Oxford English Dictionary.* The different sounds of 'ah' in Dundonian and 'aw' in Fife are used in speech preference to the 'aa' so as to distinguish them. I have since relied on the *Collins English Dictionary* (desktop edition).

Once the transcriptions were complete, there was another period of night-shift working as appropriate extracts from the transcriptions were selected and then arranged under thematic chapter headings which reflected the material gathered in the interviews.

Oral history excels in capturing the nitty-gritty detail and mundanities of life so that we can learn more about ourselves and our cultural lives. This level of detail becomes more useful as time passes by providing information on how the past was shaped by individual lives. The 115-plus individuals who were interviewed for this book are not all represented here directly. To do this would have meant diluting the part played by individual contributors so that each became little more than a disembodied voice. What is presented here seeks to represent the findings of the whole project through the voices of those selected.

Oral history is by its very nature colloquial and colourful and reflects the lived experience in a way that can complement and enhance more traditional printed sources. It is also, in my opinion, the most human, inspiring and enjoyable way to engage with our shared history.

2

SEASONAL RURAL EMPLOYMENT

―――――――――

While the central theme of this study is the soft fruit fields of Blairgowrie, in this chapter we will consider this subject alongside oral history evidence across a wide range of seasonal and rural employments. This will help to illustrate the wider rural landscape within which the berry industry operated to give us a more nuanced understanding of this time and place. Geographically, the area covered in the present study extends across Perthshire, Angus and part of Fife. Encompassing rivers and reedbeds, fields, forests, mountains, moors and seashore, this is a landscape which reflects a wide diversity of seasonal endeavour across both agricultural and industrial tasks. The twentieth century, the main focus of this study, is a dynamic one to focus upon. Arguably it witnessed the greatest polarity of transition: from the working horse to the space shuttle.

Collected over several decades, the interview extracts included here reflect an often rapidly changing rural landscape. The farming year is pivotal. Agriculture and estate work play a major role and their connection with seasonal labour is two-way. Without the labour, no harvest; without the harvest, no work. During the period of time covered by the interviews many heavy jobs on the land were disappearing while other forms of agrarian enterprise had already disappeared altogether. This brought many changes, as Jock McPherson explained:

Jock McPherson (b.1936)

Once they did away with the horses the farmers didn't need the same amount of workers so therefore there wasn't the same amount o people on a farm ... I mean if you wis followin the horse, you worked five and a half days a week. You covered a lot of miles in that work.

I was born at Aberlemno, in 1936, on a farm cottage where my father actually worked on the farm. It was the Flemington farm, Aberlemno. My life revolved roond farms fae that time until the time I left school and started to work on the farm myself ... I was fee'd in 1951.

When you lived in the country in thae days you never locked your doors. You went from one hoose to the other. 'Aye, it's me', 'Just come in' like. Ye ken. Family life and community life is ill-aff withoot it I would say. But times have moved on.

The production of flax was once an important rural industry in Scotland. Its subsequent decline was rapid due to the speed at which the process was mechanised and transferred into an urban industrial setting. By the 1850s, Dundee had overtaken Hull as Britain's biggest flax importer and was ahead of Leeds in being the north's foremost producer of linen.[40] During the First World War supplies of flax from Russia were cut off and this, combined with the huge demand for canvas and webbing, prompted a resurgence of the home-grown crop.[41] There is evidence for this in Angus and Fife where women workers were brought in to help in the harvest and were housed in temporary hutted camps. A similar resurgence, prompted this time by the Second World War, saw the establishment of factories to process flax in places like Blairgowrie and Cupar. Other products derived from flax at this time included cattle feed and an oil derivative that was used in paint and varnish.

The seasonal job of 'pulling the flax'[42] was one of many often done by Travelling people. In a Scottish Television broadcast made in November 1982, by which time he had retired, Scottish Traveller Willie Cameron recalled that time and succinctly described the rapid changes in rural practice during his working lifetime. He reflected on the passing of the need for certain jobs to be done in certain places at specific times of year. As an example, he recalled how flax-picking and other harvest work was replaced over time by the increased use of combine harvesters and mechanical potato-picking devices.

Retired farm-worker and veteran of the bothies, Joe Tindal, left his home in Angus in 1938 and moved to a farm in the Carse of Gowrie. He could recall the fields of blue flax flowers and the Irish workers who gathered for the flax harvest.[43] Like the Scottish Travellers, Irish workers moved around the country to find work doing various rural tasks during a season which extended from early spring into the autumn. This account also allows us a glimpse of how this crop was managed and harvested:

Joe Tindal (b.1916)

Ah started doon at Seaside [of Errol] and we grew aboot twa tae three acre o flax at that time. That wis the first time ever I knew o it being grown in the Carse.

And when would you start the harvest o the flax?

Well, it wis started usually just before harvest time, whenever it started tae ripen. If ye left it too late the seeds jist fell tae the ground an it hed tae be pulled before that, then it wis tied in bunches an set into stooks.

Was it a rough job for the hands?

Oh, it wis. It weren't a good job, let's pit it that wey. We hed Irishmen that stayed in the bothy. It wis them that did the flax … . All we hed tae dae wis pit it oan the carts an in lorries for the mill … it usually went tae Proctor in Blairgowrie.[44] Thir wis a big flax mill there which cleaned it, dried it an everything.

43

An wis the work piecework?
Not where I wis. The Irishmen wis there for the summer. It wis jist abut the feenish o the flax when I got there. The salmon fishers would tak a turn … they pulled some o the flax too, tae help folk out.

The Powrie family were well known in agrarian and fishing circles around Abernethy and the Rhynd peninsula of Perthshire. Cecil Powrie was akin to a modern-day entrepreneur, developing the system of bag-net fishing for salmon as well as recruiting workers from the coast of Wester Ross. It was in Gairloch during the spring of 1988 that, echoing what Joe Tindal described, Cecil shared some of his memories of how seasonal tasks often dove-tailed, with workers moving from one seasonal occupation to another:

Cecil Powrie (b.1913)
Away back in my young days, salmon fishing fitted in very well with agriculture. When the fishing finished it was just before the potato-lifting time, the tail-end of the harvest, and then thir was all the ditching and hedge-cutting that had to be done on farms. There was any amount of work available – turnip liftin occupied a lot of the men, and then there was the potato sortin. The potatoes were all lifted, put intae pits an they'd aa tae be dressed. Thir wis a great lot of salmon fishers workin aa winter at the potato-dressin, for seed ye see.

Seasonal work embraced other crops which have since fallen away. Brought up in the Dundee housing estate of Fintry, John H. Beaton MBE became a champion cyclist before he channelled that tenacity on the road to find his business acumen in later years. As a founder chairman of Kolfer Plant Ltd he made his fortune hiring out equipment for the oil industry. Much earlier than that, John more than earned his keep at the sugar beet lifting, berry picking and tattie harvesting. It was only in the more fertile soils of the east that beet could be grown successfully and Fife was the centre of this industry in Scotland. The Cupar factory imported beet from the likes of Angus, Perth and the Lothians, as well as Fife and, for a time at least, the crop supported a large workforce:[45]

John H. Beaton MBE (b.1937)
Now, there was another seasonal job you did?
Oh, the sugar beet. I didn't do that too often, fortunately, because it was really sore work. You know, sugar beet are like turnips and that's really heavy work, bent over, lifting them all the time into the same tattie baskets.

The plough had gone through and distributed them all out of the earth, but you'd to pick them up, put them in the baskets, then throw the baskets onto the back of the horse [and cart]. Tom Pate we went to, every time. Same farms. They were a good farming family. To my knowledge, they're still there yet.
So how long did the sugar beet last for?
I think about a couple of weeks, but there again there was no break because, if you were at school, you were going up there every evening and to a lesser extent Saturday and Sunday.
Whereas with the tatties?
You got a school holiday. I laugh because it used to be that those who were at Dundee High [fee-paying school] never went to the tatties and they took these weeks and make a skiing holiday. They got the same break, whereas us council house tenants were at the tatties …
A different world?
That's right.
So was there a different reason you were working for the money at the tatties and the sugar beet?
… [it] was to help fund my cycle racing because I needed a calibre bike and gear and to travel to events, because a lot of the

bigger events were Edinburgh or Glasgow. Not that my father and mother were skimping me, but they didn't see sport, other than kicking a ball, as being worthwhile … . My predicament was when I became a competent cyclist, time trials were on a Sunday morning and … I was doing Bible class. I'd to sacrifice the Boys' Brigade for the cycling.

David Wilson came from the same village (Kilmany, Fife) as world champion racing driver, Jim Clark. Both were born in this tiny village of maybe 100 of a population. David became a sixth-generation blacksmith in Kilmany and also a world champion farrier. He was awarded World Champion Farrier in 1985 after a tournament held in Calgary, Canada, which opened the doors to the rest of the world for him.

David and his wife, Mairi, gave up of their time to be inter-viewed in November 2017 and January 2019. They were the perfect hosts. David told me about the sugar beet:

David Wilson (b.1937)
How was the sugar beet harvested when you were a boy?
Well, somebody would go up and lift it by hand and shaw it, then left in pairs aw the way up [the field] and then it would be loaded. It wis aw done wae whit ye cawed a shyuck, which was a blade and it had a hook at the end [tailing knife]. Ye jist kind o hooked it up and cut it, and put it back down again.
What they cry a tapner in Angus?
Probably the same thing, yeah.
So that would be quite a sair job on the back?
It would be, and when it wis wintertime it would be cauld, wet and miserable. And beet would take a lot o pu'in. Ah think they had a 'plough' on the horse … and it would go down deep and ease these – lift the beet up, you know, so as they weren't actually pu'in them straight out the ground …

They're a different shape fae neeps?
Oh aye. They're like a [big] parsnip, kind of longer and thinner.
*And did Fife have this tradition o sugar beet cultivation, because
they established the mill at Cupar?*
Oh yes, because sugar beet wis grown right throughout here at
one time. But Ah think it wis used as an alternative crop at one
time, but the tonnages wis never quite as good as what it wis
down in England, where they were gettin better weather and
things like that. Ah think this is why the Cupar sugar beet
factory closed.

Another contributor, Bob Wilson, a retired fisherman from St
Andrews, who was born in 1926, used to cycle to Cupar for back
shifts at the factory. The additional money provided an important
boost to his income during slack times at the fishing. Caddying
was another job often done on a seasonal basis by fishermen. James
C. Robertson remarks how this greatly broadened their horizons
and, for some, provided a means of escape.[46]

The history of salmon net fishing is a complex one which could
easily be the subject of an entire trilogy. My own involvement with
the processes associated with this occupation was boosted by the
opportunity to put to sea in a fishing coble off the Angus coast, at
Usan. Being out on the water in the coble, on a sublime summer's
forenoon, was a tremendous experience. I remember I made several
attempts to take some photographs but, even in such ideal conditions, it proved difficult to steady the lens of my medium format
camera when the gentlest of waves rocked the flat-bottomed boat
as the Pullars wrestled with their nets. The wild salmon landed by
the Pullar family was valued as one of the best of our natural
products and sought out by top chefs to grace the finest menus.

Abernethy had a population of 852 in 1891 and at this time the
chief winter work was in hand-loom weaving, while the salmon
fishing on the Tay filled the summer vacuum.[47]

Getting ready to go to the salmon net fishing was arduous in itself and Tib Johnstone described for me the domestic scene immediately prior to the start of the Tay salmon fishing season:

Tib Johnstone (b. *c.*1914)
Just in the early 1920s ah used to help ma grannie to fill the fishin poke, as sh'd speak aboot. She used to cook all weekend – potted head and griddle scones, jam and as many other things … . Aw the blankets were raked out. I think their sheets would maybe be washed half a dozen times aww the time they were away. An Ah mind there was very often a pig killed – aw the grand hams hanging up in the ceiling.

All the fishermen had a kist in these days – a big wooden chest, and all the blankets and the like and their clothing, they were all put in their kist … Arch Bett, a contractor,[48] came wae his horse and cart and picked them up. They were taken down to Ferryfield and the fish boat would collect them there and deliver them to all the different lodges [bothies], where the men were workin …

Funnily enough I was married on the fourth o February, and a lot of the guests that were there hed tae be away an be ready efter twelve o'clock when the fishin started [for the season].

Cecil Powrie provided this insight into the scale of this industry when he was a child:

Cecil Powrie (b.1913)
When I wis a boy I actually saw, comin out of Abernethy village, we counted fifty-odd men with only their kit bags on their back, going down to Ferryfield on the River Earn. It was a ferry and all the boats were tied up and the men taken across to all the stations on the Tay … for six o'clock Monday morning.

In tradition gleaned from both sides of his family, the late Tom Jarvis Jnr shared his recollections of this hardy breed of men who started work on the Tay in early February and would sometimes have to break ice on the river to negotiate their cobles through the water:

Tom Jarvis Jnr (b.1936)

It was a hard, hard life they had in those days. And especially in the spring o the year, in February and March when it was hard frost and blowin a blizzard. Ah've heard ma father say he'd come in after a shift an his jacket would be frozen solid. He tried to take the buttons off, it just broke. And the next morning, when it had thawed out, there wis just a big tear across where it broke … . Oh, it wis a different world.

Born in 1900, Errol resident Jock Christie was a giant of a man and one of the oldest informants I interviewed. He had started work straight from school, aged 14, on a farm nearby, at Mains of Errol. I sadly only managed a short interview with Jock, when he was 87 years of age:

Jock Christie (b.1900)

Ken, thir usetae be a feein market in Errol days syne. They fee'd them for the hairvest when they came off the fishin. They did the reeds cutting an they gaed fae the hairvest, the boys oot o Errol. That wis their livin: fishin, cutting reeds and the hairvest. When the [Great] war started that was aa stopped. It wes jist laddies they got syne tae dae the fishin. Ah wis only fowerteen when it started. Thae wis bad years thae. Thir wis nothing but young lads or oldish men left. They taen aa the roadmen off the roads fer tae work on ferms, an aa the lorrymen oot o the toons. But the Second War, they widnae tak men off the ferms; they were exempt … . Aye, it wis a hard life Ah'm telling ye. Some o

them wis only gien a pound a week … . Ah mind when Ah got
married in 1927, … Ah'd five pounds a month. So y'il ken hoo
ye could live on that.

From the mid-1920s there arose a tradition of migrating to the
Tay from Lewis, in the Outer Hebrides, and especially the small
island of Scalpay, Harris, where a surplus of men meant that many
could not find work with their own local fishing boats. The young
women of the island also travelled south, often for hotel work in
places like Pitlochry. The young people worked through the season
then returned home for the winter months. The Hebrideans were
fondly recalled by Tom Logie when I spoke to him in 1987:

Tom Logie (b.1904)
Thir was a lot o fine hardy lads came down from the north –
from Harris and Scalpay and Stornoway and all these places.
Bailie Melville at that time used to go away up north and
engage them, about New Year time. He came to enrol them, the
day after the New Year Ah think it was.

Estimates of the numbers of islanders who made the journey
south have varied: as many as 200 in one case, although that seems
likely to be an exaggeration.[49] There is no doubt about the contribution they made, however. The Hebridean men were favoured
on the Tay because they were resourceful and steady workers; they
knew how to handle boats, and had the strength required for
rowing the cobles that were used in salmon netting before fibre-
glass vessels replaced wooden boats and engines replaced oars.

Angus Morrison, from Laggandoin, Scalpay, arrived in Perth
as a young lad, in 1942. Making the journey south must have been
an experience in itself. With lengthy ferry crossings, bus and train
travel it was a veritable marathon. Angus told me how, on his first
trip to the mainland, he had seen both a horse and a train. Both

were novelties to him. Of the two, it had been the horse that made the stronger and more lasting impression. Angus, who went on to be an inspector in the police force, possessed a superb memory honed for virtual total recall. When I interviewed him in Perth, in 1987, he revealed the following insights from hard graft:

Angus Morrison (1925–2008)

I was down in Newburgh, at a bothy there, and we worked the sandbanks. The sandbanks could only be worked at a certain state of the tide, and we had to row from Newburgh out onto the sandbanks once they became exposed. We worked the sandbank until the tide came in and covered it again and, of course, it was a bit dicey. It was never a good posting. People who were down to Newburgh knew that they were not going to the best part of the River Tay for fishing. But, against that, you also had the knowledge that they considered you good enough to send you down to work the sandbanks. Because there was a lot of rowing involved and as far as the gaffer was concerned there was also a lot of sound judgement needed. If you left it too late you were up to your knees in water before you drew in your last net, so you had to judge it very fine indeed.

Tom Jarvis Jnr (b.1936)

The station is the bit you sweep with your net. Ye can own more of the river, but your station is on a certain point, an you have what you call a hailing[50] – a gravel beach somewhere on your station where you bring the net in and land your coble. Really, your station consists of aboot a three or four hundred yard stretch from up river to this gravel beach, and usually through a deep hole in the river, if there is one. It's preferable because [the] salmon will slow up if they come to deep water, and probably be there for a tide or two.

As Newburgh man Jackson Bett explained, the fishermen had to take what work they could find outside the fishing:

Jackson Bett (b.1908) •

In older days, before my time, they took jobs in winter, breakin stones as piecework – so much a cubic yard. Some, not many, [later] went to work in the linoleum factory in Newburgh. Reed cutting was done mainly by foremen with the Tay Salmon Fishing Company. Maybe a farmer hired a man to cut reeds, and then they used to cut salt grass. Farmers used that for thatching stacks and as bedding for cattle.

When I interviewed retired gamekeeper Tom Logie, in 1987, I discovered he was among the last men alive able to recall the time when reeds were cut by hand with a sickle. Tom had formerly worked in the centuries-old orchards that prevailed in the Carse of Gowrie and when the seasonal work there finished, at the end of September, he went on to the reeds. It was about November that the blade came off the reed and it became like cane:

Tom Logie (b.1904)

My first year at reed cutting was 1918. My father was cuttin reeds and I'd go behind them, and carry [the cut reeds] ashore to the banking. At that time they were paid about six bob a hunder. That was terrible work for that. You hed a short day, going away at eight o' clock in the morning and finishing about three or four in the afternoon, in twilight. Sometimes my father had two hundred bundles: he was a devil at the work ...

And in my young days, when I was at school, he brocht in salt grass. He'd two boats and he used to go oot on a Sunday an anchor them. When the tide went doon, the boats were left ... and all the salt grass there was used for the thatchin stacks.

According to Adrian Hodd,[51] salt grass was also added to the farm stacks. Squads of up to twenty men worked at reed cutting. Some of them would wear old thigh-length leather sea boots to deal with the glaur, as well as perhaps an old stocking (sock) up to the elbow of their cutting arm to prevent scratches. Tom Logie remembered that carriers used a burden rope to carry bundles of reeds which were about three foot in circumference at the base. Here, oral history testimony is supported by the written record. In the *New Statistical Account* for 1837 it is reported that expenses involved in cutting, binding and carrying the reeds out were three shillings and sixpence to four shillings per 100 bundles, with the rope yarn being furnished by the proprietor. An acre might average 500 bundles and each bundle would be 36 or 37 inches in circumference. For thatch, the best quality reeds could gain a return of one pound five shillings per 100, and for covering drains, another common usage, about fifteen shillings per 100.[52] However, payment failed to keep pace with inflation and over the decades, for the cutters and carriers, the monetary rewards could be derisory. Latterly, the reeds were cut by a machine resembling a combine harvester which had the effect of reducing the workforce to only a few men.

Before the advent of myxomatosis[53] Abernethy men would often supplement fishing work with rabbit trapping. Only certain families did this, as stalwart of the Scots tongue and local farmer Henry Kinnaird told me in one of many interviews. Unusually, on this occasion he spoke in English:

Henry Kinnaird (b.1913)

The rabbit trappers were Abernethy men – the Doigs, Scobies (also MacPhersons). Some did dyking or helped with a fencer. The Doigs, who killed for us, came and offered a rent to [trap] for the season; half when they started and half when they ended. Some paid by the couple and sold as complete to rabbit dealers who took them from the trappers and sold to shops [game dealers]. The rabbits were put on a train to the Midlands or London. Dealers supplied hampers and the trappers took their week's kill to the station and packed them in the hampers. They got five shillings or seven shillings and sixpence a couple and there were up to thirty couples in a hamper.[54]

In the 1930s, seasonal workers such as salmon fishermen were ineligible for the 'buroo' in wintertime and they could only collect it in the summer if they were unemployed. John Barrie (b.1912) recalled that a boatman's weekly pay started at two pounds one shilling and eightpence. At that time this compared well to agricultural wages which were in a slump:

Helen Kay (b.1907)
When the fishing finished ... they just had to look for a job anywhere. Ma father used to go round the farms an it was always the nearest one to Errol he tried first. And he used to get a job. Then, of course, when it came on that it was more difficult, the jobs began to get scarce and ma mother used to be quite worried about it, wonderin how she wis going to manage. By that time I was just old enough ... and me and my sister went out to the tatties. It wasnae very much money. I think it was one shilling and sixpence we got for a day. That was the money at that time: times were very poor.

Helen's husband Sandy (b.1900) recalled that men from Newburgh in Fife often crossed the Tay to cut reeds on the Errol side. Others went off to shoot wildfowl and pigeons, simply to pass the time before they went back to the fishing.

At one time, coastal netting for wild salmon was a highly lucrative business. The ruined bothies that can still be found intermittently round the Scottish coastline, especially on the east coast, provide evidence of this. At the turn of the nineteenth century commercial salmon fishing[55] employed about 1352 men and the industry was worth over £140,000.[56] These fixed nets, known as fly nets or stake nets, were usually found running seawards from sandy beaches in an arrowhead shape. Bag nets were often at the end of these. This was a different type of fishing which relied on flat-bottomed cobles that moved over the nets to enable the crew to inspect them. As previously described by Angus Morrison this work demanded skill and physical strength. At Boddin Point in Angus the two types of fishing existed. This was unusual for a rock station.

According to their former director, Jonathan Stansfeld, whom I spoke to in 1988, long established merchants and salmon fishers, Joseph Johnston & Co. Ltd of Montrose took on about thirty additional workers during the peak season. The founder of the company, Joseph Johnston, had been a salmon tacksman who had moved north from Berwick-upon-Tweed in 1826. The company can still be found listed in the same America Street yard in Montrose as in a directory for 1885[57] and this may be taken as an indication of the robust state of the industry during this period.[58]

On a number of occasions I visited the Angus coast to gather evidence relating to the material culture of this fascinating netting process. One cold, late-February day I found retired salmon fisherman, Bill Nicol, at home in Inverkeilor. Born in 1912 and raised at Ethie Haven, Bill had a wealth of experience. The Ha'en was itself once a salmon station and base for sma line fishermen, including two of Bill's uncles. Now a coastal retreat, Ethie Haven is reached by taking the back road off the main thoroughfare, then a rough track and finally a short walk in. On reaching a rise in the road the roofs of the houses suddenly appear and its location, at one end of Lunan Bay, gives it a distinct otherworldliness. Nearby, I was able to visit the Red Castle station where stakes were built into wigwam shapes for the winter close season. This construction allowed air to circulate and they were also raised off the ground to prevent the wood from rotting. Stake nets running into the sea were once a common sight at Lunan Bay. As Bill recalled, they tended to be about ten feet high by six to eight inches in diameter. This fascinating extract describes the skill involved in selecting the best wood for the job and the strength and acumen needed for this work. Nothing was wasted:

Bill Nicol (b.1912)

The number of stakes depended on the length of beach and number of heads.[59] It was larch that was used, the best larch coming from mountain sides where there was a lot of rocks: really rough. The company selected the trees before they were cut and [the trees] came down here with the bark still on, so the men had to peel them with spokeshaves. This was very easy if the wood was green and sapping, but if you let it dry then it was difficult. The bark went to light the bothy fire and the men had to point the stakes using an axe. Larch trees from Fasque estate[60] were the best for stakes in my time. They were the strongest and could withstand the big waves.

How did they get into the foreshore sand?

This was what we called 'plantin the net'. They had to be in a straight line and you went down at low water. They were planted every four yards; some people put them every three yards.

Until about 1950 we used a tool called the gurl – about six feet high by nine inches diameter. The last few feet being pointed iron. It was best done with six men, three on each side, working the gurl back an forward. The man got a stake over his shoulder ready for planting, while the gurl was put down about three feet into the sand. Each stake was pointed like a pencil and as the men pulled the gurl out quickly the stake was driven in before the sand closed in.

Bill recalled that when his uncle was at the sma line fishing he often dug for bait in the sands.[61]

During close season some men were kept on for net mending, which was done with hand-carved needles made from hardwoods such as oak and beech. Others went further afield for out-of-season work. Bill's father had quarried road metal near Ethie Mains farm while other men went to the potatoes, to bulwarking at Montrose on the North Esk, or to the mussel beds on the Back Sands of Montrose.

Before the Second World War, David Dick of Ferryden had been at the salmon fishing with Johnston of Montrose, at their Lunan bothy. He became a railway man in 1939 but could well recall the times he was at 'the rake':

David Dick (b.1908)
Fae the brigh right down near tae the [Scurdie Ness] licht-hoose wis fu of lovely mussels. We used tae rake them wae a rake wae a long handle an they usetae come an pick them up fae Gourdon.[62] Ye got wan an six for a bag, fit ye caaed a murlin at that time.

Terms used by Johnston netsmen and not found in any dictionary include the stang or wooden pole that provided leverage to the janker when raising a bay coble a matter of inches so that the boat could float in very low water. These flat-bottomed, clinker built, salmon cobles were latterly hauled in and out of the water by tractors. Before this it had been done by manpower alone.[63]

Bill Nicol's comments about larch trees being used at the salmon fishing brings to mind another seasonal outdoor industry: forest work. In 1878, Perthshire's forests were estimated to provide employment for 2000 bark peelers. At that time the workforce was mostly Irish and included children as well as adults. The heavy rains which are common in Perthshire at the beginning of May would have surely meant their 'rude huts' provided very uncomfortable accommodation. Oaks of between eighty and 160 feet were felled in the late 1870s as the price of bark for tanning leathers in tanneries had slumped due to foreign imports.[64]

According to correspondent and Cairngorms legend, the late Affleck Gray, Travelling folk also gathered pine cones which they then took to nurseries where they sold them, in bushels, for kilning and winnowing. The womenfolk also worked in nurseries, weeding seed beds and lining out transplants for future forests.[65] The Birnam School Logbook for June 1877 reported that the 'attendance considerably reduced this week, with several of the children having left for oak-barking and other employment'.[66]

School logbooks often provide useful information about the occasional jobs that were available in a given locality and this included valuable estate work. Children absent from Kilry School, Glen Isla were reported to be at game beating on the local estate.[67] Potato lifting may well have been the main exemption from lessons each October, but it was not the only option. Kinloch Rannoch School in 1939 reported: 'Permission for four girls to attend grouse drives at Auchleeks on Friday refused … as the headmaster considers that the work was not of national importance and could easily be done on a Saturday if the employer's chose.'[68] Absences from the Royal Grammar School, Dunkeld, in the late 1870s and 80s reveal that pupils were often withdrawn from school for temporary jobs such as herding, to act as message boys or to go to the 'hounds'.[69] By 1916 it was commented that child labour was becoming more prevalent and breaks in attendance more frequent.[70]

In Scotland, grouse beating did not become an organised activity until the 1880s. However, by the turn of the century we find evidence, for example, that even a small town like Brechin could support three game dealers in addition to the butchers' shops. This serves to illustrate, to some extent at least, the local economy. Perthshire too had a large stake in sports on its estates, as illustrated in this extract:

Helen Jackson (1915–2015)
In the late 1920s and early 30s my sister and I used to go down to the station at Perth to watch the London train because it was great entertainment seeing all the people frantically trying to get everything on the train: all the porters in their caps and uniforms – pushing long barrows loaded up with luggage. It was all so hectic.

I remember during the grouse shooting season, all the toffs coming up to shoot on the Perthshire moors. The Glorious Twelfth of August was a great day and [people] would alight at all the little stations to the north of Perth as well.

It was not uncommon for lairds to hire entire trains for transportation of their guests and beaters, along with luggage, horses and dogs. Lock, stock and barrel, the retinue of one shooting family alone might easily comprise a lady's maid, nannies for the children, two pantry maids, two kitchen maids, two housemaids and two chauffeurs.[71]

Men on hill farms followed a cyclical round of seasonal jobs which included cutting bracken and hay, lambing, clipping, dipping, and cleaning out hill drains.[72] At Buskhead Farm in Glenesk the old cash book entries reveal how labour was pooled for seasonal tasks and regularly often included glensfolk, such as the local mole catcher, who would multi-task to fulfil the required workforce.[73] In the estate economy there was always a variety of outdoor tasks to be done including drainage work, gardening, planting, fencing and repairs to drystone dykes.

Documentary sources provide useful information on the make-up of rural communities. In Angus, at time of the *Third Statistical Account (1950–68)* there were only 126 permanent residents in the large upland parish of Lochlee, which covered an area of ninety square miles. Meanwhile, an old grainy photograph of the outdoor staff of Invermark Lodge from around the same time reveals a headcount of 27 men.[74] In 1872, Horatio Ross stated that the forest there had provided employment for seven or eight men as shepherds when it had been given over to sheep. This compared to 14 permanent ghillies, a figure that rose to 18 to twenty in the stag season. Another source quoted twelve permanent men and 16 to twenty seasonal. Willie Orr has estimated that with seasonal jobs, such as deer ghillies and ponymen, nearly two temporary jobs would exist for each permanent one.[75]

Trevor Royle writes eloquently about the ghillies' and stalkers' deep knowledge of flora and fauna and of the landscapes in which they worked and lived. He highlights how they put this knowledge and experience to use in service of both conservation and of the seemingly contradictory pursuits of hunting, fishing and shooting.[76]

By an act of serendipity, while writing this narrative I encountered taxi driver, Ian Robertson, who had worked for five years as a seasonal deer ghillie. Off the cuff he answered some questions from me about this way of life:

Ian J. Robertson (b.1952)

The deer ghillie's job is to look after the ponies, look after the saddles (the deer saddles) and then follow the stalker out on the hill, wait until the stalker gets a stag and [then they] will be radioed to come in with the ponies; come and gralloch the stags, lift them onto the ponies, lash them down and head back to the yard.

What did they do before there were [walkie-talkies]?

They used to set a fire and when the ghillie saw the smoke then he knew it was time to go and pick up the stag.

At the time of our interview, Ian said that estates were returning to ponies rather than argo-carts or quad bikes. The shooters preferred them and using ponies was more ecologically friendly. It was evidently very tough work: a ghillie out on the hill might walk anything from 15 to twenty miles in a day. Bleeding feet, blisters and getting soaked were all part of the job:

> **Ian J. Robertson (b.1952)**
> [A deer ghillie] needs to be physically fit anyway, and a hardy bugger. Strong, because you've to lift these stags onto the pony's back – and they're anything between 14 and twenty stone. You use the lie of the land to help you get the stag down the hill and get it on the pony's back, but you've got to watch the antlers, because the ponies are nervous of the antlers.

A certain amount of hardship was part of the attraction of stalking, be it wading through burns or arduous walk-ins to remote corries. John MacKenzie believed those who weren't out on the hill by six in the morning were 'sleepy soft-potato fellows'. A grand breakfast was not de rigueur with him. Instead victuals consisted of coarse barley scones, a kebbuck-heel and Adam's wine. 'We never dreamt of any pocket pistol',[77] he wrote.

After gralloching, whether done by the ghillie or the stalker, the innards of the stag were left out on the hill for carrion. There is controversy over any blood sport but recognition too that deer numbers have to be controlled because of the impact they have on fragile habitats by, for example, destroying new growth. Moreover, this activity continues to serve a vital lifeline to the local community by providing employment and, consequently, bolstering the viability of facilities such as the village school.[78]

Other estate-related activities deserve mention. Angling provides seasonal employment for a number of workers and again bolsters the local economy by bringing in valuable business for

B&Bs, hotels and pubs, garages and local shops. Seasonal occupations associated with angling include the river ghillies and water bailiffs whose numbers, when added to those figures for employment connected with salmon, would make up a fair number.

An unusual and often forgotten job is that of the deer watcher. Living in isolated hill bothies these men endured a spartan way of life. Primarily there to monitor deer numbers, they also kept herds from straying into neighbouring estates, sometimes with the use of dogs.[79] Adam Watson was kind enough to give me grid references for watchers' bothies from his own personal experience while John Kerr has investigated deer watchers in his researches on the Atholl estate.[80]

Industrial activity is another important aspect of our rural history and evidence of the types, processes and migratory pattern of the associated workforce can be gleaned from a number of sources. Prominent geological features, such as the Highland Boundary fault line, as well as old quarry workings marked on early one-inch Ordnance Survey maps, provide a visual guide into this industrial heritage. Craigie, above Glen Almond, is shown on a 1927 map as an old slate quarry.[81] Dig a little deeper, as local historian Thomas Wylie has done, and one learns that Glenalmond once supported a workforce of between thirty and forty men, some of whom were migrants from the slate quarries at Ballachulish, Eastlake and Cumbria. Alongside the skilled slate quarriers were the labourers, whom Wylie recalled 'came for many summers' from Skye. He continues, '[They were] crofters from Sleat, who earned as much as possible in the working season and went home in winter – men of sterling character, the best type of Highlanders'.[82] One informant, John Cameron, told me about his father, Edward, who worked at Craigie. In a photograph John had of the workforce, which pre-dated 1914, it was possible to count 52 men in the group, standing and sitting in front of the only building which served as both office and tool store. Photographs like this are often very hard to come by but when they are available can provide valuable, often unique, information for us to consider.

Earlier than Craigie was the exploratory work to open a lead mine in Glen Lyon. This work was done by miners who migrated north with pack ponies from Leadhills in Lanarkshire. Papers authenticating this can be found in the private Atholl Archive at Blair Castle.

In a thorough technical study of the brick and tile industries by Graham Douglas and Miles Oglethorpe we learn that the process of tile working was a seasonal occupation, beginning in the autumn with the preparation of the following year's clays.[83]

As with the slates, which were carted from Craigie the six and a half miles to Methven Station, the railways also assisted agrarian improvement through the transportation of primary building materials such as, bricks, tiles for draining and lime for the land.[84]

School leavers often found employment as brickworks as this tended to be an unpopular job and consequently fairly easy to secure. Chic Milne left school in 1937 and, at 14, he cannibalised parts from old bikes to cycle to his first job at 'Pudgie' [Puggieston] brick and tile works near Montrose.[85] There was no protective clothing, no washing facilities and permission was needed to go to a dry toilet which, he recalled, was 'just a hole in the ground with a wooden plank across to sit on'. It was a 44-hour week, including Saturdays, and payment worked out at a fraction over eleven old pence per hour.

Prior to firing, the bricks were wire-cut by a machine that resembled the insides of a piano, as Chic explained:

Chic Milne (1923–2017)
When this clay cam doon tae the cutter it wis pushed through these wires tae form bricks an that made ten bricks an it shoved it ontae a wooden board. The men, one at each side, would lift

the board off the cutter, ontae a barra. An when there wis fifty
bricks on the barra I had tae run doon tae the airin sheds.

The lads took turns at wheeling the barrows to the drying sheds
and Chic estimated that he and another lad, working together,
would get through about 10,000 bricks a day:

Chic Milne (1923–2017)
We usetae run back an forrit, back an forrit … that wis my job
at Pudgie. I spent two years there and went on to serve my time
as a bricklayer … . But, Ah tell ye this, outwith that it wis
slavery because the clay all hed tae be cut and transported up wi
big bogies like whit they used in the pits, on what they call an
'endless chain'.

Chic stayed in the industry and went on to become a gaffer and
site agent.

Before Chic's time, in 1904, young women worked in a brick
kiln at Kelty in temperatures of up to 150° Fahrenheit, handling
5,000–6,000 bricks daily: a pair of bricks could weigh twelve
pounds. For this they were paid two shillings and threepence a
day. This was better money than the girls who worked at the
pithead of coalmines, but less than the males who laboured in the
brick-fields and got four shillings and fourpence per day.[86] The
description of convicts labouring at the brickwork in Dostoevsky's
book, *The House of The Dead* (1860) might give us an idea of what
this work was like. With a six-mile walk to and from work, on top
of making bricks by hand, it was considered the hardest of any job
at the Siberian prison.[87]

Iain Smart spent the summer of 1967 working as a schoolboy
labourer at the Aberhill brickworks in Fife. The close proximity
to blaes or colliery waste meant Aberhill made composition bricks
rather than the clay ones described by Chic. Iain went to Aberhill

with his friend, Alec Birrell, and recalled that their job interview at Aberhill was considerably warmer than anticipated:

> **Iain Smart (b.1949)**
> We'd both gone down before the school broke up and asked the manager if he had any jobs going. He took us to a kiln door, which had just been opened, and he says: 'Stand in the entrance'. We stood and the heat coming out was something we had never experienced before. We could feel our hair singeing. But we tried to stay as long as possible to impress him. He said: 'It's okay, you can come out now'. We got the job.

As recalled by Iain, the women employed here were mainly stacking bricks. Potential employees were also often sent up by the local Labour Exchange, but this work proved too gruelling for many:

> **Iain Smart (b.1949)**
> They normally didn't stay long at all. You didn't work there unless you had to because it was hard labour. I just about died after day one. My hands swelled up, same as if you'd been labouring on a building site. The first week is always the worst, when your muscles aren't used to it.

Brian Melville was a school leaver, in 1974, when he secured a job at the nearby enclosed Denbeath brickwork. While Aberhill was coal-fired, the Denbeath kilns were gas-fired. Many industries have their own folklore and Brian explained that one of his relations believed that the new German machinery at Denbeath would mean 'Aw your men will be wearing white coats because it will be so clean in here'. Brian's actual experience was somewhat different:

Brian Melville (b.1956)

It wis filthy. Ma eyes, ears, mooth – wis fu o this black stoor.
The air wis fu o dust an it wis cold unless you wir on the
kilns … . Clay came in by lorry frae Cults.[88] It wis like big
rocks an ground in two huge grinding machines powered by
diesel. These things were huge, like the Mills o God.

I'd happy times there an met some people I'll be telling ma
grandchildren aboot. I learned tae drink strong [black] tea, in
dirty, filthy, cracked mugs, as there wisnae a fridge an the milk
wid o been honkin. Some o the crack wae thon boys wis fierce.

3
LIFE AT THE TATTIES

Potato work often came hard on that of the grain, especially if there had been a good summer. In the 1930s and 1940s the 'tattie working' involved a much larger pool of workers than any other harvest on the farm, outwith the berries. In areas such as Fife, most farms had at least three or four fields given over to potatoes. When it came to fieldwork and collecting memories of both the potato work and soft fruit gathering there were similarities and, also, reminiscences were often juxtaposed.

There has been a long tradition of migrant Irish men and women crossing to Scotland for seasonal work. They often had to endure extremely difficult, inhumane living conditions and their footprints can be found right across our agricultural landscape. They are represented here, in particular, in connection with the potato industry. Evidence of their presence can, however, be found throughout the historical record wherever hard workers were needed: the hydroelectric scheme construction being an obvious example. The textile mills of Dundee also drew significantly on the many Irish people who had settled there: a number given by Norman Watson to be one-sixth of Dundee's 90,000 population in 1861.[89]

The Irish pickers were an important part of the story of the tatties in Scotland. In this chapter, in terms of the oral material, their role is represented only by those who encountered them, rather than the men, women and children themselves. Migrant

Irish workers have left few life histories or autobiographies to give an insider's feel of what their lives were like. However, those that have been published are significant contributions and in terms of the hardships encountered can give us a sense of the true experience. Donegal-born author, Patrick MacGill's[90] personal knowledge of being a migrant worker provided the inspiration for much of his writing and he can be said to be their chief witness. After him, Sean O Ciarain who came to work in Scotland with a potato squad from County Mayo, in 1947, has described the impoverished life in no uncertain terms. Ingenuity was the partner of necessity and old bags or sacks which normally held potatoes doubled up for bedding, to keep draughts and rats out of the holes in their bothies, or even as cover against the rain:

> We cut them up and wound them round our legs like puttees for protection against the early morning dew, which saturated the potato fields and could soak a person to the skin in minutes, and the pickers who laboured in their knees in the wet stoney earth wore them around their lower limbs like the bandages of an Egyptian mummy.[91]

From the oral record and closer to home, Irish migrant labour in Perthshire was recalled by James McLaren, then a farmer at Dargill, outside of Crieff:

James McLaren (b.1912)

I always remember the Irishmen. They were really hard workers and could beat us for a day's work because they were used to cutting the peat in Ireland – used to using spades. So they came across here and made light of the work we thought was hard. I mean digging the potatoes by hand.

I've seen them hacking up dreels of potatoes with a small, three-toes graip, and they'd dig in tatties, green, and they pushed this graip in behind and shoved it out with their knee – two dreels at a time – so that they backed up a dreel and the women came on behind, lifting potatoes, putting them into barrels. Near all the potatoes in those days went into barrels for some reason. [These] held twelve stone o potatoes and they just flung them into the carts an [they were then] carted … away to be graded at the tattie merchant's store. Sometimes they left the seed out and let it green, and kept the seed separate … . So that introduced a lot of Irishmen all over this area of Muthill and Crieff. When they finished digging the potatoes we got them to stay and help us with the harvest.

The three-pronged graip, referred to here by James McLaren, had slightly flattened prongs and had been commonly used in lowland Scotland since 1800. Later, drill ploughs came to be used for opening drills for the tattie pickers.[92]

In the 1930s and 40s tattie pits were common on most farms, where the storing and cleaning of potatoes was carried out in the same way: the freshly dug potatoes were tipped into the prepared pit and farmhands would cover them with straw, then earth, in order to form a protective seal from the weather. Pits could be circular or triangular in shape and of various lengths according to the acreage harvested.[93] Examples of completely underground pits, resembling small souterrains, were still to be found in recent times in places such as Glenesk in Angus.[94]

Potato merchants usually rented the land from a farmer so the crop and production was his responsibility while the farmer may have supplied straw for the potato pits as well as carts for driving the crop off the fields in October, after the harvest.

Care was taken at every part of the process. In his fine book, *Around the Farms*, Dan Imrie writes about a tool called a herp being used. This was like a six-pronged graip – though some examples could have more than six prongs – with a marble-sized ball on the end of each prong so that the potatoes would not be punctured or damaged when lifting and loading the potatoes onto the dressing-machine.[95] A riddle, with female workers on either side, was used to ensure all foreign materials were removed before the potatoes were channelled into two waiting sacks, which were suspended from hooks at the end of the machine. This system enabled continuity: as one sack was filled and taken off the second was being filled. This was hard physical work and the heavy lifting meant that young boys were seldom involved in this part of the process.

By the 1960s, in rural parts of Perthshire, many of the tattie squads comprised labour from nearby villages including Almondbank, Bridge of Earn, Methven and Stanley. The labour was mostly made up of women and children and it was by now less common for the local squads to be run by gang workers.

In October, schools in Angus, Fife and Perthshire were given a fortnight's working holiday to support the potato harvest. Known as the 'tattie holidays' they were often looked upon with a measure of foreboding:

Mike Henderson (b.1963)

I started going to the tatties, probably when I was about seven or eight, I think. Went there with my friends, [my] brother, and [I] did that until I was about 15 or 16, so quite a number of years. I can't say I enjoyed it that much to be honest. It was pretty tough. You know, you would get up about half four, maybe five o'clock in the morning. And your mum would be up before you in fact. [She'd] make you sandwiches for your lunch when you were there. And you did sort of pray that it would rain that day [because] … if it did you got a day off, you didn't go. But, having said that, the money was fantastic.

Mike reached the fields in the farmer's horsebox, which was pulled by a tractor. He remembered that the farmer came in from just outside Kirriemuir and would go round the town collecting the squad who would then pick potatoes all day, weather permitting. The squad were picked up before first light and, in Mike's recollection of those days travelling in the horse box, 'would comprise around twenty pickers'. It was two weeks of solid work, often in very cold weather and was not work for the timid.

Others, such as John Beaton, got to the tattie fields under their own steam. John had vivid memories of his time at the tatties:

John H. Beaton MBE (b.1937)

As I lived in Fintry, on the north-east boundary of Dundee, I opted to go 'private' and cycle to Tam Pate's farm up the Powrie Brae – past the Black Watch Monument. We took our packed lunch and received a much better rate. This was back-breaking work for a twelve-year-old in 1949. The hardest part was moving the baskets of collected tatties up over the high-sided horse-drawn carts.

The carter threw the empty baskets back down, but if you didn't manage the height of the throw you had to gather all the tatties again for another attempt. In your dreel there would be ten to twelve baskets gathered for each circuit of the cart. We worked all day, eight hours, with only a half-hour lunch break, in all weathers. The kids now think life for them is tough! The biggest cheer was when the whistle was blown at the end of the day … . Thankfully our bike ride home was mainly downhill. But you were knackered!

The woven skulls or tattie baskets, when loaded, weighed about one hundredweight and it took a strong back to lift them all day. Mike Henderson recalled being allocated to help with this but said that, as most of the pickers emptied the baskets themselves, he often 'stood around doing nothing'. This was about 1979 or 1980. Dan Imrie remembered that most of the pickers, presumably to save some of the heavy work, first put their picked potatoes in a pail they had brought from home before transferring them into the skulls that the farmer had supplied.

Adults worked a 'bit', children a 'half bit'. A 'bit' averaged six to ten yards, paced out by the gaffer who adjusted the length according to the number of pickers in his squad. Rather than work by progressing up and down the drills, the pickers worked across the field. This streamlined the process and meant the pickers didn't have to change position so often. As one potato merchant put it to me: 'A woman at the end wis ay at the end'. In Kinross-shire, the stepped-out measurement – the length of a dreel assigned to each picker – was called a 'stent'. 'The stents were marked out with pegs and the tractor digging the tatties came along, then it was a rush to pick up all the tatties before it came round again.'[96]

The 'picker's piece' varied over time, as the following extracts demonstrate. The first dates to the 1970s:

Mike Henderson (b.1963)

[Your mum] would make sandwiches up: jam, meats, ham, and you would maybe get some fruit, biscuits. I seem to remember Swiss Roll was a favourite … . You would take maybe a can of Coke or juice and tea or soup in flasks. So it was like a picnic. Forced labour mixed with a picnic!

Compare this to the following extract, relating to the post-war years, and this response to an interview question about the tattie bus:

Anne McDonald (b.1946)

The tattie bus? Everybody wis manky. Ahbdee wis manky. It wis early in the morning of course and Ahbdee hed been tae Wallace's [pie shop][97] for their rolls, wie just butter on them [and there wis] singin on the bus. Some folk hed a mooth organ and a boy wid be playin on that …

Ye jist got oot the bus and ye had yer ain pieces wae ye, bottles o water, ken that; nae juice, nae lemonade. Bottled water! *What were yer pieces?*
Usually jist butter an jam or something. Butter wae sugar sprinkled ower it an wrapped up in a bit o paper, usually newspaper or something. On the bus, wae yer bottle o water, [you'd be as] happy as Larry.

For many being at the tatties was their first taste of real work and it often left an indelible imprint on their mind:

Mike Henderson (b.1963)

The work was pretty hard: back-breaking. I didn't tell you about my fingers swelling up. My fingers would swell up in the evening, after you'd picked potatoes, because you were bashing these potatoes with the ends of your fingers so the whole finger would swell up. I think it was a reaction to all the cold and the punishment.

Mike Macfarlane (b.1956)

It wis awright as long as it wasnae too cauld. There wis wan day Ah actually hed tae say, 'Enough's enough'. Ken, ma fingers wir aboot drappin aff. And the guy wis gaun back hame onywey, an he dropped me off.

Anne McDonald (b.1946)

Oh, the tatties wis murder; it killed yer back. Ah wis at Logie, so ye got picked up in the morning there, an [then] awa oot tae [the Carse of Gowrie]. Ah remember on tap o this hill. It wis like the sun wis jist comin up and ma fingers wir numb, and the boy hed jist cam doon the dreel, the tatties wir there an ah the lassies in yer class at skail started pickin: ken the thing [the skull] wis there an ye wir just pittin tatties intae it. Then ye went tae the skail for yer dinner. Cos they laid on a skail denner for ye, so the hall wis [open] for ye tae hae somethin tae eat. It wis like soup an pudding, somethin like that.

Ye got a holiday, a working holiday?

Well, they said it wis a holiday, did they? It wis a holiday. But ye needed a holiday when ye come back! That's the memories I hae, but they wis good memories though …

What state were you in after the day?

Well, ye were young, so – but the next day ye used tae feel yer back aching. An ye couldnae go hame and hae a bath. Ye had tae go tae Miller's Wynd [the washhouse]. Thir wis nae baths [at home] so ye jist washed at the sink.

Did ye wear gloves?

No, nut, nut. Nae gloves. Hands were manky: black hands and nails.

Sometimes, just a few words or a choice expression can best sum up a particular experience. When Mike Macfarlane describes the 'absolutely Baltic' conditions he recalled from one occasion when he was sheltering with others inside a van, having their piece, we can readily imagine exactly what he was experiencing. For others the tattie experience was just too much, as Mike's school friend, Brian Melville, honestly recalled:

Brian Melville (b.1956)

Ah didnae even lest half a day. Ah lasted twa oors at the tatties. The boy said tae us – Ah cannae mind his exact words but it wis somethin like: 'Here's half a day's money, now fuck off an tak yer girlfriend wae ye!' That's whit he said tae Mike cos we baith hed long hair like lassies.

That wis terrible. It wis the maist punishin thing Ah'd done in ma life. Ah didnae ken whit tae expect. We got pitched in at the back o this tractor gaun along howkin aw the tatties oot. An these women and aw these bairns that hed obviously done it fer years, ye wanted tae see them, the rate they usetae go at.

Of course, Ah'm bent doon pitting tatties in a basket an efter twan oors Ah wis knackered. Ah could hardly move. So that wis it: packed it in. Ah'm no kiddin! 'Ah cannae do this', Ah says.

Earning money was a necessity for many of the pickers who therefore had no choice but to put up with the harsh working conditions. Every field would have a gaffer, employed by the grower or the farmer himself, and the gaffer had the authority to dismiss any person who was unfit or not pulling their weight in the drills. It was not uncommon for shirkers to be told not to come back: there were plenty of others eager for the cash.

Recruitment for the farm squads was usually done by word of mouth and often the merchants' foremen would do this simply by speaking to a couple of women in the nearby village. Other times an advert would be stuck on a newsagent's window or the local post office, giving a telephone number to call to find out about available work, and those looking for work would also often contact the potato merchants directly. Adverts were being placed in local papers as early as the mid-1950s. *The Courier,* a broadsheet which had employment columns on its front page carried adverts for pickers, for both the berry picking and tattie lifting, and these would appear near to the start of the season. The advert would include details such as the name of the farm, the date work would begin and details of any transport laid on, such as pick-up points. The pick-up points were often given in local nomenclature, e.g. 'the Big Tree, Methil':

Mike Macfarlane (b.1956)
Up at the Toll Bar [Methilhill], usually the vans would come past [there]. And if they didnae have a full squad they would stop and say 'Are ye engaged?' sort o thing, and ye'd jist bale in,

tae whaurever ye wir gaun. Usually ye hed tae wait till the end o the week, mibbe Thursday or the Friday, an go up tae the boy's address in Methilhill and get yer money, sign for yer money. And [then you'd] get yer wee brown poke wae money in it.

Tattie buses were more commonly used for squads coming from the cities, like Dundee, or the mining villages of west and central Fife where the workers were travelling further. As this next extract shows, transport came in all shapes and sizes:

Mike Macfarlane (b.1956)
Tell me about the transport tae get there?
It wis usually auld vans. There would be post office vans in ma mither's time, when Ah wis a bairn and no auld enough tae gaun tae the tatties masel. Thir wis guys hed Black Marias and things like that. Auld black polis vans got sold, and GPO vans. And there would be a couple o benches doon the side and awbuddy rattlin aboot in the back o…a bare van: it wisnae too safe. Ah dinnae think ye would get away wae it these days, for sure.

It is certainly true to say that more haphazard modes of transport, such as described by Mike, or an old lorry with canopy and seats made from bales for the pickers to sit on, would have been far more common before Health and Safety regulations came into force.

Another important source of labour for the tattie farmers were the Travelling people who would stop at the tattie farms on their seasonal flit across the country in search of work. After securing work with a grower they would set up camp alongside the dreels. They brought their own transport, sometimes old or secondhand vans, and their arrival would bolster the numbers in the local squads. It was not an uncommon scene to find small parties of Travellers brewing up by the dreels, on an open fire made from tattie shaws. In other places the farmer or grieve's wife would also have brought down a pail of tea for the workers at break times.

There was usually adults and children working in the fields, the latter working a smaller section, a 'half-bit'. Heavier work, such as emptying the full skulls, would often be done by regular farm-hands or the stronger men among the seasonal workers. As Dan Imrie commented: 'it took a strong back to lift these all day'. Given the long hours of work, the short breaks that were allowed – gener-ally two – were keenly anticipated. During these breaks the tattie pickers, as with those who went to the berries, sustained themselves with banter and fun which was mostly, but not always, in good humour. Given the harshness of the work, it is understandable that sometimes things got a bit out of hand:

Mike Macfarlane (b.1956)
You wouldnae get up to much devilment at the tatties?
Bloody sure we did! Ah mind, it wisnae actually us that did it, but we wir perty tae it wan time – There wis this wan guy drivin the tractor, wan o the ganger's men like, and he wis an absolute shite o a boy. He wis jist makin things awkward for fowk, gaun too fast and aw the rest o it, an he thought it wis funny. So wan o the Methilhill boys buried a great big boulder in wan o the dreels and this thing came along. It wis wan o the [machines] wae a metal conveyor on the back that the tatties came oot (fae and then up ontae) this double trailer thing. The metal bars that made up the conveyor belt wis aw stickin up at angles [after hitting the boulder]. And, he hednae switched the engine off before he started knockin at this thing, an wan o the rails fae the conveyor belt came up an hit him in the brainer. We thought it hed killed him; thir wis blood aw place.

He hed tae be taen off the field like, an taen tae hospital. But he could o been killed.

Tempers did sometimes get frayed, as Mike Henderson recalled:

Mike Henderson (b.1963)

Well, there was the local bully. He was universally disliked – this guy – and he seemed to take a dislike to me for the whole two weeks of the tatties. Eventually, I had enough and snapped. I think he threw a potato at my brother, and that was it.

I ran after him and there was a scrap. It only lasted a few moments but you did get egged on a little bit when I first started. He was pretty much disliked and everybody had [had] enough of him. People said 'We'll do a bit for you, pick potatoes for you, if you carry on a fight with him'.

I wasn't really into fights so that was it. [It was] at the end of the two weeks and solved the problem with bullying … . We finished that day. I wished I'd done that at the start.

That was the only incident I can think of. The rest of the time it was pretty laid back, apart from the work. The work was hard.

Alongside the harshness of the work and the disputes, there was also humour:

Mike Macfarlane (b.1956)

Melv went wae us, Rodge Kinnear, Gary Cooper – Ah remember us aw gaun tae the tatties thegither. Ah dinnae regret ony o it. Ah thought it wis good fun. Ah mean, it wisnae good fun while ma fingers wir drappin aff, but ye forgot that stuff. Ye wir daen it wae yer pals. It wis a guid laugh, guid crack, and some o the boys ye wir workin wae wir absolutely hilarious. That's hoo ye got through the day.

There was little, if any, special clothing for the tattie work although the more regular squad members who came from rural areas and knew what they would encounter usually took their own wet weather gear. One former tattie merchant described this later group as 'sensible country people' who came in 'their grandfather's ex-army coat'. In his opinion, it was the 'ne'er-do-well' element who came to the fields ill-attired or lacking appropriate clothing to see them through the day. The reality was often that families simply could not afford to kit themselves out properly, as Mike Macfarlane explained when I asked him about the clothes he wore to the tatties:

> **Mike Macfarlane (b.1956)**
> Onything that wis auld and ye wirnae gaun near again; ony jeeins that hed the knees oot o them or whatever; jist anything ye wirnae gauna wear again … auld buits, ordinary buits or shoes, because again, that's aw ye hed. Ye didnae hae special ootdoor gear or onything like that.

According to one insider it was more difficult to get good squads together by the 1980s. The reason he gave was the diminution of the work ethic. However, as he himself admitted, there was more to it than just that. From the 1960s, often out of necessity, more women had gone into full-time work and so were no longer free to pick. Increasing mechanisation also played a part and soon began to have an impact by disrupting the calendar of seasonal occupation which had hitherto provided continuous employment for the seasonal workforce. Generally speaking, this was also a time when people were striving to improve their standard of living. Where possible, women were increasingly keen to move away from the hard, often dirty, manual outdoor work on the land, opting instead for jobs, increasingly full-time, such as those that could be found in the emerging retail industry. Those who could do so were also often choosing to go on to further education or to train for vocational professions, such as nursing or teaching.

In May 2004 I went to interview David Sinclair who was at that time one of the best-known farmers in Perthshire, and Scotland. He was a man with many strings to his bow and had been a seed inspector and grower, as well as chairman of the Potato Marketing Board for most of the 1980s. I hoped our interview, on his farm in the Braes of the Carse, west of Dundee, would give me a farmer's perspective on the tattie work. During our interview, what came through very clearly was the respect he had for the hard workers in the squads that came to him. He remembered many individually, including the parents of Olympian Liz McColgan (*née* Lynch) whom he held in high regard.

David also provided this interesting insight into the change-over from horses to tractors in respect of the tattie work:

David Sinclair CBE (b.1922)

The young lad that was on the third pair [of horses], Bobby Soutar, he got a tractor to drive. Then we put on another tractor. And, even then, I was still drivin the first pair [of horses] myself. Because really, what killed the horse wis the wee grey Fergie. [At that time] we grew a lot o tatties and you needed [the] horse to drill and double drill, various things like that [which] the tractor didna master [early on]. But it masters it now.

There was no power lifts or anything on them then for drill ploughs. No cabs. It was just a bloody tin seat and you put a bag on it: different world!

4
BERRYOPOLIS

Compared to the tattie picking, interviewees had fonder memories of working at the berries. The time of year was one important factor. The summer months of the soft fruit harvest were apt to raise spirits whereas the October cold associated with going to the tatties was more likely to deflate morale. That said, the berry picking was often done by the same groups of people and with the same intention: to earn money to pay for essentials. In this chapter we will consider how the Scottish soft fruit industry around Blairgowrie developed and hear from some of those who went to the berries each year.

Blairgowrie and its soft fruit industry owes much of its success to James MacKenzie Hodge, a man from an area which, at that time, fell into the adjacent burgh of Rattray. He was always proud of his family connections to Blairgowrie. In his lifetime, Hodge was a respected and successful lawyer as well as a local politician and fruit grower. He was the author of numerous articles on the subject of growing raspberries and a slim book, published in 1921 and now very difficult to come by, called *Raspberry Growing in Scotland*.[98] In this volume he charted the origins and development of the industry, which was focussed in Blairgowrie, its environs and Aberuthven in Perthshire, for a period spanning the late nineteenth and early decades of the twentieth century. The lens has been put to extremely good use here, and the generous number of black and white photographs in *Raspberry Growing in Scotland* offer us a near unique window on this world at that point in time. It is an extremely useful resource for ethnologists, researchers and general readers alike.

Following the professional path taken by his grandfather and father, Andrew Hodge (who like his two brothers has gone into the legal profession) reflected on J. M. Hodge's contribution:

> **Andrew Hodge (b.1958)**
> I've read articles which said [J. M. Hodge] observed fruit growing wild in the district and thought perhaps it could be grown commercially. That's not to say there wasn't strawberry fields and raspberries grown in private gardens [for sale] before that. But what he did was to get people to plant acres of raspberries, albeit [a] small [number of] acres. ...Despite being a lawyer, he'd [an] enormous interest in agriculture ...
>
> From memory, the newspaper [advertisements] used to say Keay & Hodge, Fruitgrowers, Blairgowrie [and] I think the first soft fruit merchants [in Scotland] would be [that firm with offices at Union Bank Buildings,] Blairgowrie from 1897.[99]

Before opening the Blairgowrie office, the solicitor's firm had been established in Dundee, in 1893, by Mr William Keay and Andrew's grandfather. Their role as fruit salesmen was then added on, as the fruit business became established:

> **Andrew Hodge (b.1958)**
> ... The clerks would be keeping legal records as well as, in the summer months, keeping ledgers of the movement of fruit from the fields to the [railway] station. So we would act as an agent and ... not just look after our own fruit, but [also buy in from] others. And, for many years I think the biggest merchant in the district would have been the firm of Keay & Hodge.

The early side of the business grew up in Rattray?
That's correct. That's where my grandfather came from and he
perhaps knew people best there and people trusted him. He had
no capital in those days. He encouraged people he'd known all
his days to do this. Such was their faith in my grandfather's
ability, they followed his advice. One of the things that
happened was that lots of people prospered. …It wasn't just a
case of one man in town making a lot of money and seemingly
doing well: everybody prospered. The town prospered. [The]
people that supplied [the berries and] the pickers prospered, so
a lot of wealth grew from what started in the 1890s in Rattray.
*Why was this part of Scotland particularly suited to raspberries in
particular?*
I think it was the light sandy soils that warms up, [the] good
climate and, perhaps, [the] lack of frosts after the spring.
*From my amateurish perspective I would imagine that the fruit
business could be quite risky due to climate and labour force?*
I think getting pickers was a problem from day one. The
evidence shows that they tried everyone from prisoners of war
[and] industrial schoolchildren, to scouts, ladies[100] … I mean,
some of the dorms were well-furnished with iron beds and
bedding, piano. But yes, getting labour was a problem.[101]
Getting weather conditions right [too]. And some years the
market was very low and little money made. So you have to be
in it long-term and you have to save in the good years.

The firm got behind Blair Estates Company, which set up
a very large camp [for pickers] at Essendy. So that would be a
major plantation of fruit with dormitories built for respectable
men and women to come and stay over the summer. So I
would think [it would be] in the early 1900s, with the backers
behind Blair Estates Company (of which my grandfather was
one), that the industry took off and began to receive attention
nationally.

Initially, Essendy pickers were almost exclusively female and hired through the auspices of the Scottish Council for Women's Trades in Glasgow. Any female pickers intending to avail themselves of the new accommodation provided at Essendy had to provide character references.[102] In the language of the time, this was done to attract a 'respectable class of berry-pickers'. Inducements to attract the most suitable pickers, *circa* 1904, included payment of the return rail fare from Glasgow to Blairgowrie of six shillings and eleven pence. The pickers came from trades such as box-makers and domestic servants: jobs that were traditionally slack during the summer months. The basic rate of piecework at that time was a halfpenny per pound of fruit. Board and lodgings had to be paid for, but could not exceed six shillings. The pickers started work at 5am when they were given a cup of tea and slice of bread and butter, for which there was an extra charge. They were fed on the premises: eggs or fish for breakfast, soup and beef for dinner. A plain but wholesome diet with all the food supplied by merchants in Rattray. Saturdays and Sundays were usually days off and drives and picnics were often organised to relieve the monotony. There was also the opportunity to attend church for those who wished to do so.[103] We can assume employment at Essendy proved an attractive option for the Glasgow women from an *Evening Telegraph* article (July 1903), which reported that the Dundee workers who had gone to Blairgowrie had returned to the city without finding employment.[104]

Later, in 1945, Gothens Farm introduced its own travel incentive to attract and retain pickers. A certificate was provided which attested that the bearer was a bona fide fruit worker and which, when surrendered, entitled the bearer to a third-class return fare to and from Blairgowrie.[105] A fee of one shilling was paid by the picker to register for this travel ticket and that sum was then refunded once the contract had been fulfilled.

In the 1950s, the prevailing culture of encouraging pickers to

1. Roger Leitch interviewing Sandy Stewart with the portable Uher reel-to-reel recorder in a glade at Silverburn, Fife. Probably summer 1983.

Courtesy of Martin Anderson

2. Farmworkers at portable threshing mill, 1930s–40s.

Courtesy of Hodge Archive

3. Portable threshing mill, 1930s–40s.
Courtesy of Hodge Archive

4. Workers busy at the potato machine,
Gothens Farm, between the wars.

Photograph by D. Wilson Laing, Blairgowrie
Courtesy of Hodge Archive

5. Workers by potato dressing machine, Gothens Farm.
Courtesy of Hodge Archive

6. Potato workers beside Meikleour wood.
The storage pits can be seen in the foreground.
Courtesy of Hodge Archive

7. Moor Field, Gothens Farm. J. D. Hodge (standing).
The field was reclaimed from an area of rough
woodland for the war effort.

Courtesy of Hodge Archive

8. A group of children with empty potato sculls.

Courtesy of Hodge Archive

9. Postcard of Gothens Fruit Farm, Meikleour, between the wars.
Courtesy of Hodge Archive

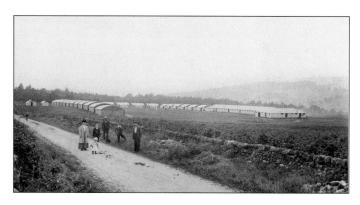

10 and 11. Photographs of the 'tin city', Essendy, early 1900s.
Courtesy of Hodge Archive

J. M. Hodge & Son, Gothens Farm,
BLAIRGOWRIE.

CERTIFICATE TO BE SURRENDERED IN EXCHANGE FOR RAILWAY TICKETS AT REDUCED FARE.

To the Booking Clerk at...Station

.... Railway

Please issue in accordance with the special arrangements which have been made with British Railways to
Bearer ....
whom we certify to be a bona-fide Fruit Worker, one Third
Class Return Ticket to BLAIRGOWRIE, on payment, at
time of Booking, of a SINGLE FARE for the Double
Journey, plus fractions of One Penny.

Signed..

No. of Ticket issued	Fare

Signature of Booking Clerk..

Date.................................

This Form to be Retained by the Booking Clerk.

12. Certificate authorising rail ticket
discount for fruit pickers.
Courtesy of Hodge Archive

Gothens Farm, Blairgowrie

FRUIT SEASON

The Gothens is three miles from Blairgowrie and the pickers' dormitories are convenient and nearer the bus route. All buildings are now sub-divided into small dormitories to give more privacy, and modern sanitary and ablution facilities are available beside them. It is essential that the new W.C.'s should be kept clean and in good order.

A Hot Plate is provided for cooking and there is a shop nearby, where food can be bought, but there is now no Canteen. There are also numerous vans calling at the farm.

The accommodation is for women only. Dormitories or cubicles sleeping from 6 to 14 people can be reserved for a group of friends, provided that the whole party applies together in good time. You must, of course, bring blankets and utensils.

Pickers are paid at N.F.U. rates per lb. picked, and the season normally begins in mid-July and continues during August. There is not so much accommodation as formerly and preference will be given to those who will definitely stay to the end of the picking and who can fill a whole dormitory.

Please fill up the enclosed Engagement Form/Forms, giving your own name and address and the names and ages of the rest of your party, and enclosing a Postal Order for 1/- per person. Notice will be sent to you whenever the fruit is ripe. Do not come before you get the notice.

THE MANAGER,
GOTHENS FARM,
BLAIRGOWRIE.

13. Flyer advertising for workers for Gothens Farm.
Courtesy of Hodge Archive

Gothens Farm.
Season

I acknowledge receipt of Postal Order for
in settlement of booking fees at 1/- per head.

THE MANAGER

14. Receipt issued by Gothens to confirm the picker's engagement (as directed in image 13).
Courtesy of Hodge Archive

15. John Hodge working as pay clerk at the weigh station, Gothens, 1962.

Courtesy of Hodge Archive

16. Label which was put on the top of fruit barrels for railway transport.

Courtesy of Hodge Archive

FRUIT—PERISHABLE.
19
J. M. HODGE, BLAIRGOWRIE.

RASPBERRIES.	GROSS.			TARE.			NETT.		
	Cwts.	Qrs.	Lbs.	Cwts.	Qrs.	Lbs.	Cwts.	Qrs.	Lbs.

THIS LABEL NOT TO BE REMOVED.

17. Weigh station at *Antwerp* Field, 1962.

HODGE ARCHIVE

return year after year reflects the paternalistic attitude of the growers at that time, but it also made good economic sense. The incoming correspondence to Mr Hodge of Gothens Farm at that time shows that the workforce came largely from the west coast. G. M. Hodge kept a record of the names and addresses of loyal workers who stayed the longest. Married women would write matter-of-fact letters from Glasgow on behalf of their families e.g. Mrs Sarah Aitken of Glenpark Street; Mrs E. Marriot of Dechmont Street, Parkhead; Mrs McColl of Glendale Street, Denniston; Mrs McHendrie of Dalserf Street; Mrs McIntyre of Gemmel Street; Mrs Sweeney of Brown Street; and Mrs Walker of Glamis Road. Other letters in the Hodge Archive came from workers in places such as Airdrie, Cambuslang, Coatbridge, Edinburgh and Paisley. Mrs Barnes, writing to Mr Hodge from Fraser Street, Glasgow in May 1959 to request a placement for her husband and family at Gothens, gave details of four sons, the two older of whom she describes as being 'quite good pickers'.

A leaflet from around this time provides further useful details: the manager of the farm advertised that pickers would be paid National Farmers' Union (NFU) rates per pound for berries picked during the season (normally mid-July through August). This leaflet also tells us that there was less accommodation available on the farm than had formerly been the case and states that precedence was promised to families who could fill a whole dormitory and were prepared to stay to the end of the picking.[106]

Other groups played an equally important role in the success of Blairgowrie, including the Scottish Travellers, as Andrew Hodge explained:

Andrew Hodge (b.1958)
And have the Travelling people not picked many a berry for the industry?
The Travelling people have. They were a backbone at times

[although] they would be not enough originally. It would be locals. Travelling people came and went. But the scale of the operation at Essendy, and elsewhere, demanded dormitories (and an influx of people from the cities) … . Certainly, from my father's perspective it was mainly [from] Glasgow that we got our pickers.

…

I was brought up [at the farm] and I was out on the farm when I was home on holiday. And I used to assist the farm-workers throughout the year. I might be helping in a very small way, cutting out canes [and I'd be] having a piece with [the farm workers] when they were inside the steading. … They used to always refer to their breaks still by the terms used when the horses were rested, such as 'yoking' and 'mid-yoking'. … I remember that.

There was quite a large labour force on the farm in these days – five or six people – because of the fruit, and the farm manager or grieve sat in the shed with the head tractor-man.[107] The other workers would sit in the stable and they would of done that, traditionally, because the stable would of been the warmest place on the farm.

In the summer, I remember the preparations: from washing barrels to getting all the pails ready for the Glasgow Fair starting. And my father, always keen, looking forward to it … . Certainly the families that came year after year used to have their furniture kept in storage and it was up to the farm manager to put their furniture in the correct dormitories. And families would arrive and be there for the fruit season and be taken up from the dormitories to the fields by tractor and trailers, or walk. It wasn't far.

…

When I was a boy, [with] the Glaswegians, it would be granny, daughter and grandchildren running around. It was a summer holiday, in sunny conditions. Albeit, by modern standards, fairly primitive … but it was the summer months. It was the Glasgow Fair, July and August, so people roughed it.

They smoked heavily too. My father worried a lot that there would be a tragedy, but there wasn't. I remember Embassy fag packets and people smoking all the time, which you're not allowed to do these days with table fruit. We were lucky that there never was a tragedy … due to somebody smoking in bed and [accidentally] lighting a straw mattress.

John Stewart was born and bred around Blairgowrie and Rattray. He worked in England before migrating to Canada, where he spent ten years. His family always did their soft fruit business with George Hodge, Andrew's father, and had strong links to the Travellers.

John Stewart (b.1946)

My father had 15 acres of raspberries at Wolfhill,[108] that's on the Perth Road. Up in Rattray we had raspberries there, five acres. Never had any strawberries, it was always the raspberry trade we were in.

My father first started in raspberries about 1950–51. It was a thing at that time that was coming on. He sold all his raspberries to Mr Hodge of the Gothens. He was a buyer in the 50s. It was raspberry pulp. We never did any baskets [for table berries] it was mostly all pulp we did.

When can you mind best what Blairgowrie was like during the berry season?

I can remember pretty well back to [being] five, six, seven year old, in the 50s … . It was a busy place. Glasgow people, Dundee, Aberdeen, Edinburgh. The town was absolutely mobbed for approximately five, maybe six weeks, and it was the raspberry capital of Britain at the time, Blairgowrie.

Douglas Davidson was chairman of Walter Davidson & Sons Ltd, the largest independent pharmaceutical chain in Scotland. The company was founded in Blairgowrie in 1897, with branches in both Coupar Angus and Blairgowrie. He remembered:

Douglas Davidson (1928–2018)

You could hardly move. In fact, to give you an idea: the manager of Woolworths (Perth) lived in Blairgowrie, and once a year the directors visited each of the Woolworths' branches and did their assessment. … Now, it so happened when they [were to visit the Perth manager] it was on a Saturday at the start of the Glasgow Fair. The manager invited the deputation of directors to have their lunch in what was then the Queen's Hotel in Blairgowrie, which is in the middle of the High Street. So, of course, when they came for lunch you couldn't move in Blair … the directors came out and they saw the crowds milling and said, 'Oh, we don't need to do any market research, we'll build a Woolworths here, it's definitely needed'.

Now they could of come on any of the other 365 days and it would have been a quiet, sleepy town … . But that's how we got Woolworths in a place the size of Blairgowrie.

John Stewart (b.1946)

As far as the eye could see it was raspberry fields. And my father used to get campers, you know, they stayed in tents in those days, just round the end rigs of the fields. And it was mostly Glasgow and Dundee pickers we had.

Was there a culture clash with all the city folk arriving?

There was a wee bit at times. The Wellmeadow here, when you came out the pubs at night you could hardly get [moving] in the town with the amount of people there was. But there was some good banter. One or two fisticuffs at times. [laughs]

It was really a good atmosphere. And, I think in those days

each farm had a wee bit of rivalry to get the best pickers. Plus, I think, some of them exaggerated a wee bit on the tonnage they were getting. It was *Malling Promise* raspberry canes that we grew in those days, because in the early 50s that was the top raspberry cane. We thought that was the best one in those days, although there was quite a lot of other varieties.

How did you father hire the pickers for the season?

I think it was just word of mouth if I remember rightly. We used to get quite a lot of Travelling people because my father knew quite a lot over the years and they would [come to us] quite regular every year, the same families. And the Glasgow and Dundee people, he knew quite a lot of them. So it was the same families all the time.

… were the Travellers the backbone of the pickers?

Yes, they were in those days. Because they would come and stay right through the raspberry picking season, into the harvesting of the potatoes.[109] They stayed about Blairgowrie right through until almost just before Christmas.

And was Blair like a Mecca for them?

It was. Yes. There used to be a bit went up to the Pondfields, at Parkhill. There used to be hundreds of families came in those days, especially the early to mid-50s. A lot of them came from further north, and the islands, but they all collected around Blairgowrie really. Not only that, anybody who hadn't seen families for months [would] get all the news and they did a bit of wheeling and dealing with cars, caravans as well.

I remember my father telling me [that] earlier, before I was born, it was horses and carts they came with and they used to wheel and deal, buying and selling horses and carts.[110]

…

And there was also in the town a chap, Fender, who used to hire out bicycles. There was thousands of bikes around the town and, of course … it was quite a walk to some of the farms, so they hired the bikes for something like three or four shillings a week. You would walk round the town or out in the berryfields and there would be a bike lying there. They just abandoned them, the old sit-up-and-beg type bikes: boneshaker tyres. Nothing with three-speed gears or anything like that, just old-style bikes …

My grandfather and grandmother, they always used to go round the camps at each farm because they knew a lot of the Travellers … so they always went round to see who was staying on the farms and talk over old times. [There would be] a big fire outside at night, the kettle on, brewing tea all the time … . They used to tell a lot of ghost stories. They were awful for their ghost stories, Travellers. … My grandfather always used to tell us about the Burkers.[111] Going up Glenshee and Braemar you couldn't walk alone because the Burkers would get you. So they always frightened us with tales.

Renowned Scottish Traveller, Sheila Stewart, provided this next account of the berryfields:

Sheila Stewart MBE (1935–2014)

I was in a berry field three days after I was born, at Blacklaw. I … cut my teeth on a berry cane and grew up with the berries all my life … . It was a great thing for the people, the non-Travellers and Travellers, to come to Blairgowrie for six weeks of the year. It was a working holiday thing, absolutely brilliant. Because the Travellers could come and camp anywhere. At the end of a field or anything. And they were great berry-pickers because they had their whole families.

I was saying to John, it was like a Mecca for the Travellers.

Oh, my God, aye. I mean it wasn't just the berry picking to make money. It was a meeting for the Travellers. Every single year they came and they met. They'd ceilidhs round the fire,

and it was unbelievable the fun that went on at the berry-time.
It was great …

And would girls and women meet a lad?

That was half the function of the berries. But the Travelling
people had a funny way about them because they never went
and got married, they just ran away. If the boy kent the lassie
and the lassie kent the boy, and they 'fell in love' as they say
nowadays – we never called it that – they just ran away, came
back, and that was them married.

Those pickers who camped were referred to as the 'moor squad'.
One person who witnessed this great assembly gave me a colourful
description of what it was like. This sharp-eyed description is given
vibrancy by Sandy Stewart's fluency in Scots, his first tongue:

Sandy Stewart (b.1920)

An ye got whit they caad the Gowthens Muir [Gothens]. Hit
wis a big muir an the berryfields wis aa roon aboot it. This wis
thon bonnie bent stuff growin intae hit an all the camps wis on
hit, an hit wis like a toon! They came in thair on bicycles,
horses, cairts, motors, vans, caravans – aa kinds o things come
in thair, an that's whaur ye could deal if ye'd money. Gowthens
Muir wes oot fae Muckleoor [Meikleour] yonder on the road
gaun tae Blair. When they wir drunk, the tinkers sung steady,
playin the bagpipes aa nicht an singin till moarning. Ye'd hear
the pipes gaun aa ower an think it wis pipe bands wae them.
Some ye'd get fechtin an arguing till moarnin …[112]

Retired farmer John Henderson was born at Newlands at
Wester Essendy. He had been a clerk in a shipping office in Glasgow
before health issues saw him return to the farm.

John Henderson (b.1925)

Wester Essendy was quite a big farm at one time and it was divided up into smallholdings ... away back before the 1920s, by Keay & Hodge – who were farming Wester Essendy at one time. They saw the area was suitable for fruit-growing and decided to give younger folks a chance to grow fruit. So that's how my father came to own Newlands at Wester Essendy.

What was Strathmore like during your time with berry farms?

The Strathmore valley, as far as I can remember, was very suitable for growing fruit, especially raspberries. And I can remember all the fields round about the house were raspberries. As I say, there were five or six farmers and they had communal dormitories for berry pickers. In my young days there would be about 500 or 600 pickers at Wester Essendy. There was a waste piece of ground converted into dormitories, all tin. It was called the tin city at the time – There would be about forty berry pickers in each dormitory. And at the height of the season there was a bus ran from Blairgowrie out to Craigie, just to take the berry pickers in and out from this communal dormitory place. Just back and forwards, back and forwards ...

I remember at the threshing mills we used to take these big palliasses, they were just hessian bags, and we filled them with straw for mattresses and the berry-pickers brought their own sheets and things like that. Latterly, we got a stand-pipe, but there was no running water. There was two wells. The pickers had to go and just draw their own water until such times as the mains supply came. There was no form of lighting, just candles. Of course, they were all away to their beds before it was really dark.

Douglas Davidson describes the impact so many pickers had on his family business:

Douglas Davidson (1928–2018)

In those days [my father] closed at eight at night [in Coupar Angus] but my grandfather didn't close till nine at night here [in Blairgowrie]. So, immediately my father was finished he headed off up to Blair and I used to see the crowd, as a kid. …
For instance, the bus stop there, which is on level ground, that used to be a shopping place, and that's where all the (sorry to use the term but it's what we used) tinkers used to come in on a Saturday with their wee carties. They were all parked on the slope [near the Wellmeadow] and they frequented the pubs.

They were really going like a fair on a Saturday at that time. And many of the tinkers, they just piled in their wee carties, and their ponies knew the way, and off they went.

I always thought as a kid that this was very exciting. Because there were a lot of fights used to break out on a Saturday night and I can remember folk coming out through pub windows!

John Henderson added his own memories:

John Henderson (b.1925)

I was never much in Blair on a Saturday night but I understand it was a pretty rowdy place. All the berry pickers would just flock into the town for the evening … to let off steam and spend what little money they had.
What were the berry pickers like?
Oh, the Glasgow folk … I remember them arriving. They were all smiles. They thought they had landed in heaven really [laughter] and were quite delighted to sleep in these dormitories. It was mostly women and girls. I don't remember the men coming at all. But I don't think they made a lot of money. It was a good holiday for them, maybe coming away from the slums of Glasgow, away out to the country. The Fair Fortnight was the

busiest for others, when they came up in their hundreds.[113]

I remember my sister saying, 'I don't know where we're going to put all those folk that are coming on the buses tonight, because the dormitories are all full'. But she managed.

What were the buildings constructed of?
Some of them were just corrugated iron, some were brick, corrugated iron roofs you know ... like a Nissen hut. In fact it was during the War that the Polish Army took over the tin city and they did a lot of alterations, putting ... in ... proper lighting, [and] that bottled gas, you know. I remember they did that. But after that it reverted back to the berry pickers again.

Then, of course, the authorities clamped down because there was no proper sanitation or anything. Just earth toilets [with] no proper way for washing or anything like that. Each grower decided to house their own berry pickers in caravans [on] their own grounds and that's what my father did. I remember well one field, what they called the 15-acre field, had quite a lot of caravans on it and there was Glasgow folk originally in them ... . The Glasgow folk seemed to dry up and we got foreigners in, and they were good workers I must say. In fact, they would come out in the evening at night and work late, whereas you'd never get the Glasgow folk doing that – or even the local folk.

These foreign berry pickers would start coming in about the 1960s or 70s, before polytunnels. We never had polytunnels. [They] came in when I came out of the farm about 1982.

Margaret Miller,[114] whose husband, Wallace, was grieve at Gothens, had vivid memories of the pickers who came to stay at Gothens:

Margaret Miller (1931–2014)
I was roughly trying to count up with all the families of Glasgow

people that came. We must of had at least fifty or sixty, maybe
more for the Glasgow Fortnight. Some went away after 'the
fortnight' if they'd jobs to go back to, you know, men that
maybe had jobs. But the majority stayed. The only thing was,
some of them would go away on a Sunday night back to
Glasgow to collect their dole money on a Monday morning.
And they'd be back by Monday night for another week ...

They'd the time of their life. There was all their berry
money. So, yes, a lot of them ... . Well, Friday night was the
night for going into Blairgowrie, and they never actually picked
berries on a Saturday ... . They went back to Blairgowrie on the
Saturday night, but they'd come out on the Sunday to pick
berries because they'd no money left. But Friday night, Saturday
night, was their nights for going into Blair.[115] They were never
any bother ever, really. There was never any bother ...

And, as I say, the majority of the Glasgow people stayed
till they were finally told that the huts were eventually closing,
you know, there was no berries left to pick. But some of them
were allowed to stay on for another week. Mr [G. M.] Hodge
let them and then he would say, 'Right, the huts are closing
such and such a Saturday'.

John Stewart (b.1946)
A lot of the Glasgow and Dundee people just went round every
farm to see if they could get a place to work and a place to stay.
So you always had plenty of pickers in those days.

The city folk usually stayed round the end rigs with their
tents. There wis a lot of young people came to Blairgowrie. The
Teddy Boys [came] in the 50s, from Glasgow ... . They had the
drainpipe jeans, the thick suede shoes and they all carried sheath
knives and guitars.

Singer Sheena Wellington went to the berries as a teenager and she too remembered the flamboyant Glasgow youths:

Sheena Wellington (b.1944)

I remember the Teddy Boys ... in the mid-50s and they were
sort of [a] great amusement, wandering about with their jackets
doon to their knees and their troosers that they'd tae be poured
intae and their velvet collars. There wis a good few of them.
And, of course, Elvis became the rage and I remember going to
see *Love Me Tender* with my cousins [and] thinking, 'Oh, he's
beautiful'. That was the kind of social life we had. You know,
the pictures were all important. Televisions were in but, I mean,
we had two channels! We got a TV when I was 15.
Going back to the fifties, can you describe the appearance of the
pickers?
Well they didnae wear their best claes. It was the oldest stuff
that you were wearing oot because it would get stained. And it
didn't matter how careful you were you would get berry stuff ah
over it.

It would be dungarees for the men. ... The women very
rarely wore trousers in these days, it was skirts, but they usually
had a peenie – the wrap-around peenie – and [the aulder
women] always had their hair up in a turban.

Bairns were different. Wellies, especially if it was a wet day.
It was either wellies or sandshoes because naebdee had mair
then. You'd a pair of good shoes for the school, you'd a pair of
baffies (or roavies even) and you'd a pair of wellies and a pair of
sandshoes. That was your footwear. Baffies are slippers and
roavies are actually made of jute and people would weave them.
They were actually quite comfortable and no only that, if you
had big ones [they] could slip over your shoes and [they] gripped
in the snow ... . You wore the roavies inside but very occasionally, if it was icy weather, you'd get them slipped on ower your
shoes because the jute just seemed no to slide. We didna like it

because we liked slides. We made slides when it was frosty.

You mentioned the men having to sign on [the dole] *every day.*
Was it possible for them to take on agricultural work?

It was difficult. There was a berry bus went round later to pick up because you'd to sign on and you'd to sign on at nine o'clock or half past eight. You had to be signed on before 10 o'clock. There was a berry bus used to hang about Gellatly Street [where the Dole Office was], or no far off – because it would be spotted! I think it might of been up at the North Lindsay bus station, because there was a bus station up there at that time, and they just made their way up there and slipped on it. But actually it was a dodgy thing. They needed the money …

If you got caught earning any money, even if it was only coppers, you could be disallowed for six weeks. [That would be] fatal for a family man with a couple of kids.

Am I right in thinking that at this time more men in Dundee
would be at home?

No, that wasn't so much the case in the 50s, though unemployment was always quite high so there was always a few men. And the mills were on short time. I can remember my aunties only working three days instead of the five and a half. So, you would get a few extra women coming on a Monday or Tuesday because they weren't working. [The short week] meant they'd a greatly cut pay.

Who was looking after the bairns?

The bairns were on the bus!

If the men were working, they were working. But if they were unemployed they'd be on the bus an ah. As I said, if you were unemployed and you were getting the pittance, and it was a pittance that you got on the buroo, [then you would go to the berries]. You would occasionally get a car coming up and [this would be] the [dole] inspectors …looking for people that shouldn't be working because they were getting unemployment benefit. Naebuddy had cars, so if a car came all the fellas that were carryin their buroo cards sloped off in one direction.

Andy Fenwick (b.1964)
I can't remember the Social [Security] ever stopping the buses but I can remember them coming on a bus and I can remember them arriving at the berryfields. And I remember seeing just a load of people running, saying, 'Here's the Social!' And a lot of people would just take off down the berryfields. They'd to run as fast as they could. They must have been on the Social, claiming, and they weren't wanting to get caught. A few times I've seen this happening. The rumour swept around the berryfields: 'The guys from the Social are coming' and people who were obviously claiming benefits would run away to the very end of the dreels and hide.
So, do you think people had a greater equality amongst themselves at the berries?
… Yeah. Definitely. The people that went to the berries, I think, were all one and the same. Nobody viewed themselves as any better than anyone else. We were all there to do the same thing, obviously: pick berries and make some extra money. But you had fun as well. You would hear, in the berryfields, laughter rippling across the fields and people telling jokes and people singing.

Sheila Stewart, another sadly missed contributor, shared her recollections:

Sheila Stewart MBE (1935–2014)
When Travellers were in the dreels picking berries, would singing go on then?
Oh, that's when the singing did go on. That's when we all sung. My mother sang. I sang. My sister Cathie sang. And then other Travellers would join in …
   I'm the legacy [Belle Stewart] left Scotland. Her and my

uncle Donald, her brother. She taught me the ballads and he taught me how to sing them. And the berry time was a great time, because we used to go and pick berries but it was like a ceilidh in the field … it was like a concert every day when we were picking berries.[116]

Andrew Hodge (b.1958)

You'd hear people singing if they were happy. If the pickers were happy, you'd hear them singing in the berry drills if you were on the loading bank. But yes, you would know when the camp was a happy ship and, to be honest, most of the time it was. I think the only time things got rowdy was on a Friday or Saturday night when there was an over-indulgence in alcohol by the grown-ups.

But that would be outwith the farm was it?

Yes. The town would be noisy but back they came, usually on foot; there wasn't so much taxis in those days. They could come back and be slightly the worse for wear … and there could be a wee bit of havoc caused. But it wasn't too often. But yes, Blairgowrie certainly would be a busy, boozy place in these days …

Berry gaffer's daughter, Maureen Marra, also remembered the singing:

Maureen Marra (b.1949)

The berries would start about seven in the morning. It was really dawn until dark. And people came from mainly the Kirkton (Dundee). And whole families came, because it was always in the school holidays. They brought pieces for their dinner … something like jammy pieces, because nobody had money, [or] flasks …

Was there much singing in the dreels?

Yeah, people used to sing. You sang away because you had to

jist get on with it, kind of thing … . They just sang all the old things like *Shove Yer Grannie Aff the Bus*. Just something rousing to keep folk going while they were picking. You could hear somebody starting to sing far away and other folk would pick it up if it came down.

Singer Sheena Wellington, from Dundee, recalled from her own time at the berries:

Sheena Wellington (b.1944)

[You had] ex-army knapsacks … and you'd have your bottle of water, or juice if you were lucky, or cold tea or whatever. You'd all pile into the buses and sing all the way to Cransley [Farm]. Usually stuff you wouldn't want to repeat in mixed company. All these songs … I was the world's worst berry picker and the only way I made any money was singing during the denner hour. People would say 'Give us *The Old Rugged Cross*' or things like that.

I went home with nearly as much money as people got picking berries … we'd sing *The Lochee Boys* and that kind of thing. There weren't that many others [that] were specifically about Lochee; it was all adaptations of other songs.

Sheena is talking here about the 1950s and this was at the same time as folklorist and ballad collector, Hamish Henderson, was harvesting his own crop of vibrant oral tradition from the berry-fields. He made many fieldwork trips to the area with his reel-to-reel tape recorder.[117] In his words:

What we encountered in that drystick wood, in Jeannie Robertson's house in Causwayend, and at the Standing Stones berryfield on the road to Essendy, was this wonderful fluid thing representing the actual world of the ballad singers, a shared sensibility still artistically vital and fertile. Singers who *are* singers remake their own versions …[118]

As these next extracts demonstrate, the berries also seem to have provided an opportunity to learn important life lessons, or perhaps these are more realistically evidence of the kind of mythology that surrounds all types of communal work:

Maureen Marra (b.1949)
When you used to get your berries weighed, if you had a farmworker that was a bit mean they used to put your bucket on the scales to weigh and then they would lift it off quick so that you weren't getting the full weight of your buckets.[119]
There was sometimes fights at the – well we always called it the 'berry-up'. There was fights if somebody thought they'd been underpaid.

In fairness, pickers were not averse to increasing the weight in their pails by every dodge they could muster. Not all, but some, alluded to such tricks. A sharp-eyed weighman usually knew the likely suspects:

Jenny Burns (b.1963)
I remember the boys, not the girls, on occasions peeing in the raspberry buckets to make it heavier. But these always went for jam … they weren't concerned so much about what kind of berries were in the bucket. But there wes some of the boys used to [do that]. I never saw anyone actually doing it but they said that they used to do it, thinking that [the berries then] weighed more and they got more money.

Andrew Hodge (b.1958)

We were all sent out [to pick] when we were young at the farm, in the summer holidays … . Albeit we weren't [as] able or [as] interested as the Glaswegians that used to come and stay on the farm. After picking, and being looked after by very friendly and nice Glaswegians, we went to look after the cash. And so, along with my two brothers, we did our bit of being on the loading bank. And the pickers would come in with their pails and have them weighed by the weighmen, and then I would pay out the cash.

I remember hearing of a terrible strike that was in the *Antwerp*'s field[120] and it was very leafy canes [with this variety of raspberry cane] … . I think my grandfather came out to the farm to see what was wrong. They just sat on their pails and refused to work. That was quite a serious strike. That [one], I think, took place between the wars.[121]

What was the outcome of it?

I think it would be sorted with increasing what was paid per pound or just waiting until they came back to the fruit fields.

In this next extract, Irene Fyfe, interviewed in Dundee in 2011, shared this anecdote from her mother's berry experience:

Irene Fyfe (b.1940)

… my mother used to relate. She came from a very poor family and when she was in her teens the whole family went out to Blairgowrie and they were given … a hut or a place to hire. Anyway, they stayed there. That was their holidays, picking berries, and in the evening they used to go out to the dancehall and mum and her friends always put on gloves so that nobody would know they were berry pickers.

From a slightly later era, Joan Kettles told me of her own

attempts to avoid the scratches which were an inevitable conse-
quence of the berry picking:

Joan Kettles (b.1954)

I used to wear a pair of socks on my arms, cut holes for my
fingers to go in and sew in between to make it like long gloves.
That was to save from scratches because you didn't want
scratches on your arms when you were a young lassie and if you
were going out.

Did you wear a wristwatch?

Yes, I think I did actually, because you had to know what time
piecey-time was, and you would keep looking at it and think,
'Ah well, I'll maybe just get this dreel finished before we have
our break'. Or then the farmer would sometimes shout 'berry-
up!' [and] that meant it was time to go and get weighed
because, you know, he'd be wanting to go home.

…

I was at the berries the week before I gave birth with my eldest
one … I remember I went back again the next year to pick
berries and I was pregnant again with my next child. … [My
first] was just a year and I had her in the pram. I remember
putting her in a crate at the end of the dreel. You couldn't do
that now … . Everybody knew each other there and they would
all look out for you. But I remember trailing from one field to
another with a big pram, crates on top of it. You know, you
remember all sort of things.

Then you had to go home and light a coal fire. We had no
central heating and we didn't have an immersion [heater] so
you had to put your fire on to get hot water. You did that in the
middle of summer so as you could get hot water to give the kids
a bath and get clothes washed for the next day.

We had running water that was pumped from a spring
because we stayed in the middle of a field. So it wasn't mains

water. If you got a power cut … you didn't get running water because it was obviously electric that pumped it. So if you didn't have running water you couldn't put your fire on because there was no water in the back boiler and otherwise the boiler would burst …

Anne McDonald was born and brought up in the Hawkhill district of Dundee, close to the neighbouring Blackness Road and her account tells us more about the pickers who came out from Dundee and the berry buses:

Anne McDonald (b.1946)
Where was the pick-up point for the berry bus?
West Port, or sometime it wis the Blahky – for people in the Hahky an Blahky. Then ye wir there [until] efternin. Then the bus back – covered in berry juice. The fingers were red n that. When ye think back it wis good, [but] it wis hard. Ah that pickin, gettin stung by bees an wasps.
How did ye ken tae be ready for the bus?
People telt ye, ken, the bus will be there the moarnin, say the Blahky, at seevin o'clock or something. [And if ye] wir going ye had tae be there cos it didna wait on anybody. If ye wirna there it jist went.
Were folk turned away?
If the bus wis full ye widna o got on it. … There wis no standin on the bus; everybody wis sittin.

A younger generation of pickers interviewed for this study included Dean Tait from the Fintry housing estate, to the north of Dundee, and Andy Fenwick who was brought up in Lochee:

Dean Tait (b.1962)
There would be a place where they would pick-up and you

were up early in the morning. You got yourself down there wi no guarantee you were gettin on that bus. That was the problem. I think probably they would take adults first … certainly I made it there on plenty of occasions.

You were getting on these old buses that probably wouldn't even be roadworthy these days … . They were double and single deckers, it just depended on the farm you were going to. The condition of them was pretty much the same … . Aye, they weren't the cleanest things.[122]

Andy Fenwick (b.1964)
If you were inside the buses, they actually stank. They'd a horrible smell that was a mixture of berries, raspberries, and a kind of rotten egg smell, and I think it was with all the mud coming off people's wellies when they were going on the bus at nights. Also, berries would be splattered over the bus, on the floors and on the windows. You knew right away when you saw a berry bus that it was a berry bus.

On one occasion Andy recalled the berry bus was stolen by teenagers at Cransley:

Andy Fenwick (b.1964)
… They got halfway down the road before they got caught by the police and obviously had to bring the bus back to the farm … the kids were only about 15 or 16. They actually stole a double-decker bus!

One man I spoke to who drove a berry bus (within the law by that time) was Korean war veteran, Jim Devlin, who was born and bred in Dundee. After Jim came out of the Army he worked as a long-distance driver for the British Road Services:

Jim Devlin (b.1933)

Well, I have a Public Service Vehicle licence [from] when I worked as a corporation bus driver. This was in 1956. Actually, I don't think you needed a PSV to drive a berry bus.

Where the berry pickers used to congregate was Mid Craigie Circle [roundabout], on the Kingsway, and of course there was no traffic there at that time. It wasn't a bypass.

I was just, sort of, between jobs. I think I saw an advert in *The Courier* or it was word of mouth, I don't remember. I went to a guy up in Dennison Road. He owned a lot [of stuff, including] some berry farms, and he ran the buses. They were old Alexander buses. So I got a job from him, driving one of these buses, and it were a farm away up at Aberlemno.

He asked me if I could get a berry squad to take up there, so I sort of let it be known in the street. I lived in Charleston at the time and Michael [my son] probably spread the word … that there would be the bus available. And there was about one hundred turned up: loads of them.

I also told the other guy at Kirkton, this was my uncle, to tell people round there. So when I went there I actually had to force people off the bus, there was that many of them. [I had to] stand at the door [and] keep them off, because it was absolutely packed to the gunnels.[123]

We used to stop on the Dundee Loan in Forfar. They all wanted their crisps and their lemonade, and, of course, they crowded into this shop and the shop was sort of bursting at the seams. The young guys were just lifting everything, all the sweets, nicking everything out of the shops.

Bank manager, Heather Hay, remembered a more unconventional mode of transport from her own youth:

Heather Hay (b.1957)
I remember going to the berries when it was in Forfar and the picking-up point was the Mart … . And we got picked up in a cattle float. So it was quite exciting going in this float, as you could see out of the little square bits … and there was just a set of seats right down each side. The same ones as you see with the animals now. So I remember that. [It was] good fun.

Another younger informant, Paul Hill, was brought up in Menzieshill on the west side of Dundee. When I asked about what kind of people mostly went to the berries in his day, Paul told me:

Paul Hill (b.1962)
They had large families … children of about ten, eleven, twelve. They werenae there to play about, they were there to pick and make money, because these families were very poor … . The reason behind it in these days was paying for your school clothes, your uniform.
So you gied the money to yer mum?
You gave the money to your mother. You maybe got something off it for a treat, but it was mostly towards your school clothes. That's what it was for.

Paul Hill, like Diane Donnelly from an earlier generation, had mostly gone to pick in the eastern part of the Carse of Gowrie where there were berry dreels at Longforgan. Diane was 26 and married with five of a family when she went there to the berries:

Diane Donnelly (b.1934)
We went oot the Perth Road. We used to walk oot, past Longforgan … and one was in a pushchair. The other four, they picked the berries as well … . When we went to the berries [it] was to get the bairns' school claes. Ah bought what we needed

for sandwiches, lemonade for the bairns. Peter and I had a flask of tea [and] what was left went into a jar.

Now, at the end of the two weeks, I went and bought their school clothes and I only had to put maybe £10, £15 of my ain money to get them.

Was there any left over for treats?

They got tuppence each on Saturday.

It was a common enough sight on the dreels to see mothers who were accompanied by their very young children. Care worker, Joan Kettles, went to the berry picking outside the village of Coupar Angus and recalled her own experience as a young mother:

Joan Kettles (b.1954)

You'd a pram to push and piece bags, which was a trauchle because you'd to shift the pram from dreel to dreel. Say there were sixty pickers – that would take up thirty dreels, so you'd a lot to move to the next dreel, which could be up to forty dreels away. That was in the busier time when more people were picking.

A school tie was used by Joan to attach her luggie to her waist, with a cleek that was like a small hook or karabiner at the end of it.

Pickers normally worked the dreels in pairs, one on each side, and would often partner with a friend or one of their family. Being a solitary picker was much more time-consuming and therefore a far less attractive option.

John H. Beaton was brought up in a poor area of Lochee, in his words, 'up what you would call a pendie' with two rooms, no hot water and an outside toilet shared with the neighbours. When I asked him about the people who went to the berries, he told me:

John H. Beaton MBE (b.1937)

Oh, there were posh folk that didn't go, and there were others that didn't go because they were too lazy …

And, from a young age, you would be taught the value of money?

Well, we had none, really. At the berries, every penny was truly precious. You were excited if you went away and got a penny vantis – which was a carbonated drink. Nobody would buy it now, but it was different then. And you would even go sometimes to an ice-cream shop. And if you couldn't afford ice-creams you would buy a penny's worth of crummled wafers, [ones] that hed been broken. They sold the crumbs off! That was something different.

So was the berry money your money, or did you pool it into the family?

It came into the family. And I got pocket money then, as such. The only pocket money I had maybe.

John recalled that he had gone to the berries with his mother from a young age, twelve or even earlier. He only stopped when he became a pre-apprentice with Bonar Long in Dundee. He recalled there were noticeably more women at the berries and thought this was perhaps because the menfolk were working elsewhere during the day, or just too lazy. Young children were also enlisted to help, although this would be more for raspberries going into pails for pulp rather than the table berries. As John remembered:

John H. Beaton MBE (b.1937)

There was a lot of fun [in the dreels] and maybe people throwing an occasional clod of mud at each other. But if you plastered about too much you just didnae produce enough berries. And if you weren't producing enough on the day – because they kept a wee log – they'd maybe say: 'Oh don't bother coming back', because they'd maybe have someone who could pick better.

When it came down to it this was a business, and a well run one:

Andrew Hodge (b.1958)
I think, if the farm staff had problems with either the pickers fighting amongst each other or perhaps people hitting the bottle too hard, if there were certain families who didn't pick well or [caused] more trouble to the farm than others, then we'd mark their card and would do our damndest to see they didn't return the following year.

Margaret McMaster's mother came from a background immersed in seasonal employment which included tomato growing and potato harvesting. As she explained:

Margaret McMaster (b.1958)
… that was the way I was brought up. My mum started running berry squads. In the wintertime it was potato squads, but in the early days it was always the strawberries first in June … and berries to get your school clothes then. You had to nabble. The more you nabbled the better the clothes you got. That kind of thing.

The dictionary definition for the Scots word, nabble, defines it as working with speed and deftness, which appropriately reflects the expertise involved.[124] This definition, from an oral source, provides further evidence of meaning of the term:

Joan Kettles (b.1954)
… That was just somebody that nabbled the berries. It was like [the berries] seems to fall off the bushes into their baskets and they were up and down, up and down, weighing their buckets. You were always mesmerised: 'My God, how did you manage to

pick all that and I've only managed to pick this?' But, as I
progressed I started getting a better picker too.

From a slightly younger age group, Jenny Burns recalled happy
memories of going to the Arbroath berries in a big pink-coloured
double-decker bus. Hundreds of people were trying to get to the
dreels to make money in the mid-1970s. Luckily, Jenny's father
knew the farmer so she and her brothers always got a place. Unlike
some buses, which would return to pick up more pickers if a heavy
crop was ripening quickly, this bus did only one trip. In this extract
we can see that Jenny enjoyed the benefits of contributing to the
school uniform fund:

Jenny Burns (b.1963)
We used to buy our own choice of school uniform. If you relied
on your mum buying it then you just had to make do with what
she wanted. But, if you earned your own money you were able
to come up to Dundee and buy your own uniform that way.
And anything else?
Just usually records and things like that. Little bits and bobs
that you might not have been able to afford … . My first record
was Michael Jackson.

Other memories of the berryfields take us back to the Second
World War and just within the compass of living memory, as with
this recollection from Helen Jackson:

Helen Jackson (1915–2015)
It was the summer of 1942. I was a music student and we had
long holidays, so I went to the berry picking for the experience –
and the money. And it was an experience! I was living in Perth
and took the bus up to Blairgowrie. I had got fixed up at a farm
to the west of the town where we had accommodation in cabins

that were very spartan. But that was all part of the fun. It was basic. We were young and we didn't mind.

The gaffer knew his position and simply loved to hector the students, take them down a peg. We were just berry-pickers like the rest.

[You said before that] *somebody said that working so hard was affecting their heart.*

'Aye' the gaffer said. 'The only heart you know is being heart lazy'. I remember that. It was a snide form of snobbery because he thought we considered ourselves to be better, which we did not. He just liked to bully.

Bill Anderson, a gaffer in the 1960s, was of a very different ilk. Bill worked at the berries near Blairgowrie during his summer vacations from the University of Aberdeen. He reached the dreels by pushbike from the town and recalled his boss checking with the weather station at Leuchars every day for up-to-date forecasts as poor weather could ruin the season.

Bill remembered one occasion when two girls hassled the owner for an increase in the piecework rate, hoping for a rise to fourpence a pound from threepence. As Bill recalled:

Bill Anderson (b.1948)
And he said 'Oh, no', he wouldn't entertain it at all. So they started to sing *The Red Flag.* You heard this coming from the dreel: 'We'll keep the red flag flying high'. He didn't laugh, but I did. His quote was: 'Fucking Bolsheviks!'
And were there any strikes?
No. I can't remember. I don't know, with the owners, whether there was a certain cabal or not, to organise what price it was going to be. But, say you were keener to get workers you would put up your price a wee bit, say [if] you were needing a lot of berries to be picked.

It is clear that the berry money was vital in providing the means to buy necessities but going to the berries also provided opportunities to meet new folk and maybe even find romance:

Joan Kettles (b.1954)

I would say it was quite a happy time. A lot of the women started courting the young men who came through to the berry picking. You got to know a lot of the people. You got to know who was coming and we'd pick beside them.

Did girls from the village get off with Dundee men?

Yes! Well, if offered a better opportunity! Because the [available] village folk were very few and far between. You set your eye on [one and maybe thought], 'Hmmm, he's a bit of alright'. It didn't always last, but sometimes it did.

So you looked forward to the berries?

It was part of your life. … You used to dread going in the mornings, but it was part of your life – and sometimes it was nice going to work. You met new people, and it was better when you started getting a lad. Then you really looked forward to going to the berries, staying late, because there wasn't really anybody else going about.

As well as providing a vital service for pickers travelling to the Blairgowrie area, public transport also played a crucial role in taking the fruit out by freight transport. This was hugely important at the height of the season:

Andrew Hodge (b.1958)

The railways were here before raspberries began. But, yes, the freight traffic in Blairgowrie would be extremely important. And, I think Blairgowrie continued for longer than it otherwise might of, despite Beeching coming in later, due to fruit traffic going all over the country.[125]

In going through old copies of the *Blairgowrie Advertiser* on microfilm at the A. K. Bell Library in Perth I came upon one report of 49 wagons laden with fruit departing from Blair. This would have been at the zenith of the industry and sights like this will now be disappearing from the touchstone of personal recollection.

Douglas Davidson was able to provide this detail from his own memories of that time:

> **Douglas Davidson (1928–2018)**
> They used to muster the wagons at Coupar Angus and hitch them onto the London sleeper train. This was [wagons for] fresh fruit and the London sleeper went through Coupar Angus. Before the days of refrigeration there were long cars, slatted at the sides, and the speed of the train going [and] … a cold wind surging through them … it acted as if it were a refrigerator.[126] And they brought the fruit from Blairgowrie and put it on those trucks at Coupar Angus. I have a photograph of the Blairgowrie 'Raspberry Special' but I'm not sure where it went … . There wasn't the huge demand for fresh fruit then but, of course, there was down in London and that's why they hitched this on.

Stanley Sim was born in Broughty Ferry and moved to Alyth when he was only nine months old. His father bought over a bankrupt ironmonger's business which, in due course, Stanley took over. When I recorded him in Blairgowrie, in October 2011, he shared with me his own memories of the berry crop, the role of the Alyth railway and, especially, his uncle's jam factory which used berries that had been set aside for pulp:

> **Stanley Sim (1928–2014)**
> The only berries that went from Alyth were the ones in the baskets, that I know of. They went daily by rail. There was a

railway station in Alyth at that time, of course. I was just a boy
at that time. But I know that once the big casks were filled they
just lay in the yard. I actually never saw any of them go, but they
would go to jam makers. They wouldn't can them. The berries
that were canned went fresh to Smedley's and my uncle had a
jam factory here [Adamson's jam factory, Blairgowrie]. Their
berries went in fresh for the jam …

It was interesting, because the women washed the jars by
hand in a big tank of water that was steam heated. He was a
pernickety old guy and the jars were all wiped by hand after
they were filled. He wouldn't sell any jars that were down in the
neck[127] and we used to go along and get [those ones]. [laughs]

Most of his customers were in the Aberdeen area. They
were all north. And he put the jam in great big 17-pound stone
jars as well and sold them to hotels and bakers, people like that
who were making jam rolls and things like that … I bought a
jar of marmalade the other day and it was very down in the
neck. It would never of come out of Adamson's jam factory like
that. The name was actually sold to Mackay Brothers away
back. They're still on the go, and they were famous for
marmalade.

A funny thing about it, Uncle Dave always put salt in his
jam because he said as an illustration 'salt wis ten bob a
hundredweight, sugar wis three pounds a hundredweight'. The
more salt you put in the less sugar you needed. [laughs]

*Do you remember the scene round the station when they were
putting fruit away to the southern markets?*

Aye. There was an engine shed, a passenger platform and a
goods yard. They used the key and the loop in the bag that had
to be handed over to the driver or guard … . They were all
steam trains and funnily enough we always thought that the 'S'
in LMS was for Sim because my grandfather was the stationmaster at Alyth and he got a promotion and was stationmaster

here. His brother was a ticket inspector in Glasgow and one of the other ones was in the transport police.

I always had a great affinity to steam. It might have been wagons on the passenger train but there was a goods train came in too. The passenger train ceased about 1955 but the goods train continued after that because they [still used the trains to get] rid of a lot of the tatties after the berries. Wordie[128] was the carters. It was horse and cart at that time that used to deliver the buckets to the shop. And all the goods came by train of course: tattie baskets or sculls. We'd a lot of domestic stuff. We did a bit of sport and ammunition, not much in guns but cartridges. Lots of jam-making pans, the jeely bags and things like that.

As with any large-scale migration and people working away from home it was inevitable that there would be some criminal activity. What follows is largely taken from the experience of retired sergeant, Willie MacFarlane, and retired constable, Andy McKay, both of whom went on to serve with Tayside Police[129] after its amalgamation in 1975.

When they were interviewed, Willie and Andy were both reflecting on long careers as policemen and they shared detailed recollections of the law and order issues from their time at the berries, some of which are quite colourful. It is interesting to consider the different perspective their accounts highlight. The majority of berry interviewees understate the amount of lawlessness at the berries and any anecdotes they did share were usually dismissed as simply scuffles that followed bouts of over-imbibing.

Andy McKay joined the old Perthshire and Kinross-shire Constabulary on 12 March 1962 and was stationed at Blairgowrie from October 1963 until September 1971:

Andy McKay (b.1940)
My first impression of Blairgowrie was probably coloured

somewhat by the tales that would [be] about within the force
regarding what Blairgowrie was like during the berry season … .
It was quite an interesting place to work.
Was it perceived as a challenging place during the Glasgow Fair?
It was perceived as a very challenging place during all the berry
season! … You had this seasonal employment, which was largely
based [on] people gravitating from Glasgow, Lanarkshire, staying
in Blairgowrie for the duration of the berries. And [then] you
had overlap situations again with the Dundee holiday period. I
should of said that the population would increase quite considerably [and] you could loosely say, all hell was guaranteed to
break loose.

Willie MacFarlane joined the former Perth and Kinross
Constabulary in January 1974 and was sectioned at Blairgowrie.
He is an author of *The History of Perthshire and Kinross-shire
Constabularies* as well as being Honorary Curator of the Tayside
Police Museum in Kirriemuir.

Willie MacFarlane (b.1954)

Believe it or not, I used to pick berries even when I was in the
police. That was part of the reason they took in lodgers. In the
berry season they would say, 'Any chance of giving us a hand to
pick the berries?' And that was fine. I was on the other side of
the dreels with some people I was coming into contact with,
maybe, at my work. Strictly speaking, that wasn't correct. But I
don't think anyone ever regarded the berries as other 'employment'. I was doing that more to help my landlord and landlady.

Blairgowrie is a ghostly shadow of its former self. When I
arrived in 1974 it was past the peak but [still] there was not a
spare piece of land in Blairgowrie that was lying empty. All
berries. Even a quarter of an acre would be used. All around the
Marlee Hotel in Rattray it was surrounded with raspberries[130] –

I think that was actually the house, at one point, of Adamson the jam makers. So everywhere had berries.

…

Blairgowrie was the capital of the raspberry growing industry, and you must of heard of the tin city – Essendy. The tin city was named obviously because it was a bunch of tin shacks, but no sanitation whatsoever. And all these workers were housed in these tin shacks …

Now, there was a policeman actually stationed at Essendy[131] for … years during [the] season.

Can you remember when that was roughly?

1930s. The last one I knew was Donald Campbell who died just a few years ago. Donald was a policeman at Blairgowrie and he was stationed at Essendy. He was actually transferred. There's a force general order saying 'Constable Donald Campbell transferred from Blairgowrie to Essendy temporarily'.

And he stayed in digs somewhere near the blacksmith's shop. He was in digs there and that was his job. His landlady's house was the official police station.

When I came to Blairgowrie, in 1974, raspberry picking was still a big thing in those days, but sanitation laws meant that many places like tin city had to close down… And the people from the Glasgow Fair would arrive in Blairgowrie and, traditionally, Saturday was a day when raspberries weren't picked at all. It must have been some farming agreement but you could guarantee that on a Friday night that was when the money was spent. And the Wellmeadow in Blairgowrie was actually heaving with people up till maybe three, four o'clock in the morning. They were all transported by taxis, or whatever other way, back to their camps.

How did you police that?

With a lot of difficulty! You certainly weren't allowed to have your annual leave during the berry season.

Andy McKay (b.1940)

It was challenging, without a doubt. And it was an excellent grounding area for young police officers who were brought up to man-up the regular numbers in Blairgowrie for the duration of the berry season, which would be ten weeks, twelve weeks, by the time the berries were away. And they would be re-posted back to some other divisional stations within the Force area.

…

Part of our remit at that time was to feed the prisoners who were locked up during the berry season. You would feed them – before they went to the court – with their breakfast. If they were there over the weekend you would have to find a lunch and a tea for them and for that inconvenience and trouble you got paid … a bit of a pittance. It was, from the best of my recollection, two shillings and thruppence for each meal provided. So that was just another add-on to the traditional policing that perhaps indicated how archaic things were at that time.

Was police leave cancelled during the season?

Well, there was no routine cancelling of leave in as such that it was an operational decision, but the efforts of management at that time would be to have as many people on duty during the berry season as possible. And the ones who were able to get to their holidays in the summertime … [it] would be the senior officers, who would get first choice on the leave rota.

Willie MacFarlane (b.1954)

Blairgowrie's section, when I left, had only four or five special constables for the entire section. When I joined in 1974 we had about twenty-five, maybe thirty special constables for that same area, so there were very many more special constables. And many more members of the public were prepared to come to the assistance of the police [then].

Every crime imaginable would happen during the berry

season. Thefts were commonplace, break-ins to garages, shops, whatever. Of course, you've got to remember Blairgowrie had its own resident [criminal] population who were equally proficient at break-ins.

How were custodies housed?

In Blairgowrie police station. We had, in those days, six or seven cells … and another two at Coupar Angus.

Andy McKay (b.1940)

So, the Wellmeadow was undoubtedly the hotspot, or the busy spot, during the berry season … . It was undoubtedly a gathering point. I think, from memory, there was about seven pubs within visible distance, if you stood in the Wellmeadow and just looked about you[132] … . And, of course, at that time they all came out [closed] at ten o'clock. Inevitably you had a mix-up of individuals who would be coming out the worse of drink, … some of them much the worse of drink …

There was no restriction on people carrying alcohol about with them and it frequently happened that you got what would be known as winos, as well as ordinary hard-working people who [had taken] a drink …

If you were lying about drunk and incapable in Blairgowrie at that time there was a simple resolution to that: you ended up in the cells until next morning whereafter you would make your appearance at the Burgh Police Court.[133]

Willie MacFarlane (b.1954)

And would they dispense within the Police Court really quickly?

Oh, God, aye … and the rule was that they had to appear in court on the first lawful day. So, if you arrested them on a Thursday they would have to appear in court on Friday morning … Saturdays and Sundays were not lawful days, so it would be the Monday.

Douglas Davidson was a senior Baillie and JP. He recalled:

Douglas Davidson (1928–2018)

… in the late 50s, 60s … [we] had to have courts every day of the week during July and August because of the number of incidents. To actually illustrate this sort of thing, there was more dealt with in the local courts in those days than in Perth [Sheriff] Court.

I can remember one woman that nearly buried a hatchet in her husband's head on the Saturday night and I had them up in front of me on the Monday. You never saw a more luvvie-duvvie couple in your life. But they'd taken drink.

Andy McKay (b.1940)

Well, the Burgh Police Court was a pretty busy place during the berry season. To be honest, on several mornings of the week and sometimes on consecutive mornings you would have lock-ups from pubs [as well as] disturbances in the Wellmeadow or on the way out to the various camps which were situated, basically, in all directions from Blairgowrie.[134]

Going on to the Wellmeadow and the pubs there, did you ever have to break up disorder involving groups of folk?

Oh, you were frequently involved in that sort of thing. Aye. I mean, there were regular disturbances you would say, and it didnae necessarily all take place between incomers and the locals – or people from the district. It was very often fighting amongst themselves, particularly the Lanarkshire, Glasgow group who'd literally invade Blairgowrie for the whole of the summer.

…

How general would it be for the pickers to have their own transport?

Some did and some didn't. The ones who came from Glasgow

probably didn't all have transport of their own. They probably arrived on public transport. A lot of the Travelling families during that period would arrive in old vans or old pick-ups, which would be kept either in the end rig of the berryfield or in the field where the tents were erected.[135] Tents were also super-seded largely by caravans, old beat-up caravans, which would sometime[s] be provided by the farmer ...

Which vehicles did you have?

We only had two cars in Blairgowrie. We had a Ford Zephyr patrol car and a 1500 Wolseley all-purpose vehicle. That was the total sum of the vehicles when I went to Blairgowrie.

More in relation to larger groups, how did you make a large arrest?

With difficulty, I could add! Not always was there just four in the back of the car. Sometimes you might have them piled a wee bit on top of each other. You might have to confess to that, which nowadays might be subject to a complaint against the police. But at that time you got on with it. Frankly, they got on with it as well!

Willie MacFarlane (b.1954)

I remember, the first time I saw Blairgowrie being given a van ... thinking that would be handy to transport prisoners (and other things about, too). But before that people were thrown in the back of cars, vehicles got damaged. All the upholstery got damaged, the doors, cushions, everything. That's just the way it was. It's hard to explain ... . But in Blairgowrie you had to learn fast. *Semper Vigilo*: always be vigilant. That was the motto of Tayside Police.

The next extract, from Andrew Hodge, reminds us that for most of those who took part in any aspect of the berries, the experi-ence was a positive one:

Andrew Hodge (b.1958)

By the end of the season, and perhaps the weather beginning to turn in September, you looked forward to normality being returned. It's something, when a year passed you forgot the trials and tribulations. But it was an enjoyable, busy, happy, noisy time …

I just think of so many people being involved … I think of generations brought up from the cities and their first taste of life on the land was [a] cheap summer holiday, a working holiday. In the days of Butlin's, the alternative was to go and pick berries on Perthshire fruit farms. … I have this memory of pickers watching a wee aeroplane flying over and [them] indicating that was the farmer who owned all the land, as far as the eye could see, and that was their vision of the fruit farmers [laughs].

I … think many people in Glasgow and Dundee, and elsewhere, will just have happy childhood memories [about] what that income brought in, allowing them to have (perhaps) extras, before [the children] returned to school.

Andrew's comments are reflected in this final extract from Margaret McMaster, which also reminds us of the central importance the berry money played in family economics:

Margaret McMaster (b.1958)

The same at the berries. The flask was always there; it wasna like bottles of coke that the kids get now. It was diluted juice. You were lucky you got orange juice. Yeah, really good: happy days. I've got a lot of great memories from years ago with my mother. Sadly my mum's no longer here; she died young, at 55. But I've got a lot of happy memories and I've got four kids of my own. When I told them the stories of my growing up they were like that [open mouthed]. 'Oh you're joking mum.' And I went: 'Oh yeah, I had to pick for to get clothes in these

days … we all had to pick the berries, tatties, nabble away.
The more you nabbled, the better you got.'
Necessity?
Very. Very much necessity, yes.

5

THE GROWTH OF THE RASPBERRY INDUSTRY IN SCOTLAND
by G. M. Hodge

W̲e are very fortunate to have for our consideration this text of a talk presented to the Blairgowrie, Rattray & District Civic Trust by Andrew Hodge's father, G. M. Hodge, in autumn 1987. In his own words, G. M. Hodge shares with us his thoughts on the past, present and future for the berry industry that is central to his own family history. Within the context of the present study it provides a unique and valuable insight.

In the last decade of the nineteenth century, raspberry growing in the Blairgowrie area was only on a very small scale. In case of doubt, I should make it clear that I was not around quite so long ago as that, but got my information from my father's book, *Raspberry Growing in Scotland* – now long out of print – and various notes he left.

So far as I know, most of the rasps were grown in gardens in very narrow drills and in 1895, the largest grower with a holding of a fraction over an acre adjacent to Rattray School was a Mr James Moran, whose grandchildren are still in the district. I think my father had something to do with the tenancy, but I am not sure what it was. The field was planted out with the *Antwerp* variety of raspberry and gave yields of over five tons per acre.

I understand that my grandfather and Mr William Hovelsroud both lent a hand at times with the manuring of the field which was, in these days, carried out by one man pushing a wheelbarrow down the drill and the other forking out the dung. I think it fell to my grandfather to fork the dung.

Incidentally, I am told that it was Mr William Hovelsroud's father who originally suggested to one of the very early growers that the canes should be laced to the wires with a continuous length of twine in the same way as fishing nets are made up. Until then, one small piece of twine was used for each cane which made tying up a very slow business. I mentioned the narrowness of the berry drills. This was, of course, because room for only a man and a barrow was required. With the start of field scale cultivation, wider drills were needed to accommodate horses and horse-drawn implements and the drills became wider still in the more recent past when horses gave way to tractors.

In 1895, my father started the Blairgowrie and Rattray Fruit-growers Association. In that year, the total crop from this area was twenty tons of which the Association handled 14 tons. My father remained secretary of the association until 1904, when the new plantations at Essendy came into bearing and he was no longer able to deal with outside fruit. In 1898, he took a lease of Wellbank in Rattray. This was an eleven-acre holding and he planted it out with raspberries. He was told he was mad and would flood the market, but he carried on and later bought the field which remained in the family till a few years ago.

In 1899, he suggested to Mr David Adamson – the founder of the Ironmongery and Jam Making Business in Blairgowrie – recently engulfed by William Low – that he should buy a small farm of thirty acres in Rattray and let it out for fruit growing. My father had the ideas, but at that stage he had not the capital to put his ideas into practice without the help of outside finance. Mr Adamson bought the farm and one of his tenants was James Stewart, a cobbler from Atholl, known, I believe, as Stewart the Boot. He was a shrewd man and bought his five-acre holding for

£100 an acre, an unheard of price at that time. Before settlement date, he sold two and a half acres for the new Strathmore Fever Hospital for £700 and was left with two and a half acres at no cost and £200 profit. Mr Adamson still owned part of the farm twenty years later. As a child I remember that we quite often met him at his piggery on our family Sunday afternoon walk. I always used to hope we would not see him for we had to wait for what seemed an age while our seniors talked instead of getting down the path to the Milton where my bothers and sister and I could race our paper boats under the little bridges.

In 1900 my father leased Langbank, a field of nearly twelve acres on the outskirts of Rattray for himself and others and two years later he took a ten-year lease of 17 acres at Westfields from the Thomsons. I think that Mr James MacDonald of the Welton was the first fruitgrower to realise the necessity of providing buildings to accommodate the pickers and this was also necessary at Westfields where dormitories and a canteen were put up. The landlords saw that the venture had been successful and, not unnaturally, refused to renew the lease at the end of the ten years. The Thomsons are still large scale raspberry growers in Rattray at Westfields and elsewhere.

While the acreage under fruit had, of course, greatly increased, the really big expansion occurred with the success of the Essendy small holdings. In 1902, Blair Estates Co. Ltd was formed, the Directors being my father, Alexander Mackay, C. A. Dundee, Dr William Low (who was either the original grocery supermarketeer or, at any rate, connected with the firm) and William Keay (later Provost Keay) partner in the legal firm of Keay & Hodge which was intimately concerned with all aspects of the growth of the raspberry industry in this country.

When the company bought Essendy, it made an effort to keep things quiet until it had completed all its arrangements. This effort was not entirely successful. In February, 1903, an article in the

Dundee Advertiser said:

> The evident desire to keep the matter dark has only whetted the
> public feeling and all sorts of surmises have been heard; one was
> that one of the tenants was the actual purchaser; another that a
> wealthy Dundee gentleman had bought the estate for residen-
> tial purposes and intended to erect a handsome mansion upon
> it; a third made the purchaser an Indian magnate for his son.

The paper then proceeded to reveal the name of the purchaser and
reason for the purchase.

Some 450 acres were included when the estate was bought, but
the proprietor of Marlee Estate was worried by the thought of an
influx of wild berry pickers, though I can assure you that, in these
days, they were sober, God-fearing individuals compared with
some of the wild Glaswegians, Dundonians and Fifers we came to
know later on. In any event the owner of Marlee Estate bought
from the company 200 acres round Marlee Loch to protect his
amenity and this went a long way towards providing the company
with the necessary working capital.

One of the main objects of the Blair Estates Company was to
encourage small holdings in furtherance of a 'back to the land'
policy. To make things easy for the small holders, they were asked
only to put down a deposit to account of the price of £50 per acre
and the balance with interest at four per cent was payable over ten
years. This worked out at about £6 per acre per year over the ten
years after which the land belonged to the growers absolutely. Not
bad in an area where fruit land was being let for as much as £10
per acre at that time.

The Blair Estates Company, on behalf of the growers, erected
dormitories and canteens to house and feed the pickers, arranged
catering staff and organised the provision of respectable young
women from the cities to pick the crop, a policeman to protect

them from the amorous young men of the district and a medical student to act as doctor and look after their health.

The Essendy venture was a great success and proved that raspberry growing had become big business. To quote my father's words:

> It often happens in business as in gambling that what one man wins another man loses, and that takes half the pleasure away. It has been otherwise with the smallholdings at Essendy. Everybody connected with them has made money – the company which created them, the smallholders who worked them and the community which gave its labour and goods in exchange for their produce.

Incidentally, the crop from Essendy alone in 1905 was 189½ tons – over nine times the total crop of the district only ten years before, and the Essendy total rose to 736 tons four years later.

In 1907 Drumtogle and other farms on Aberuthven Estate, near Auchterarder, were bought for raspberry growing, Drumtogle extending to 220 acres was turned into small holdings on the lines of the Essendy experiment. James Stewart, whom I mentioned as one of the very early growers, and who had 13 acres at Essendy, took thirty acres and made it pay well, but, on the whole, it was not so successful as Essendy. Blair Estates Company, which had managed the Essendy holdings bought the Hall Farm and other companies were floated to purchase Westerton, The Arns and Shinafoot, the other farms on Aberuthven Estate when they came on the market in 1912. These latter farms were not run as small holdings and, at the end of the First War, which had, of course, made picking very difficult, they were sold to a syndicate of English jam manufacturers at the price of £170 per acre – everything included. The last fruit crop from the farms and small holdings before they were sold came to 760 tons.

After the Auchterarder farms were sold my father bought Gothens Farm of some 300 acres a few miles outside Blairgowrie and, at times, more than half that acreage was under raspberries. Up to now, I have been reporting mainly what I have read or been told about, but I stayed at the Gothens during several fruit seasons in the pre-war times and have lived there for over thirty years. Between the wars, some of the other large growers were, so far as I can remember, the McIntyres, who started at Essendy, Mr Nairn the vet, the Thomsons, who succeeded to Westfields, the Petries, John Dick the coal merchant, the Crichtons and Smedley's.

In 1930, Blairgowrie Raspberry Growers Limited, a fruit merchanting business despite its name, was started by Mr William Inverarity and now under the management of his son, is one of the largest concerns in the district.

During the 1939–45 War unlike the position in the First War when raspberries were controlled only in 1917, all the fruit was pre-empted by the Government. The allocations were made by a committee of local merchants presided over by a civil servant and fruit was sent, so far as possible, to preservers in proportion to their pre-war supplies. I was appointed to the pre-emption committee in 1946 to succeed my father and, after pre-emption ended in 1947, the committee continued unofficially to try to stabilise the price of fruit. We all told each other what tonnage we had sold and at what price. At least, that was what we were supposed to do. At what turned out to be the very last meeting of this committee, all of us, with one exception, told of our dealings. One gentleman steadfastly refused to give any figures at all. Pressed to explain why, he said, 'If I telt you what I'd sold you'd no believe me and it would be a lee anyway'.

After the last War, Dr Colin Cadman and Dr Conway Wood came up to Tayside from, I think, East Malling, to run the Scottish Raspberry Diseases Investigation. It was much needed. The original variety of *Antwerps* had long passed into oblivion and so had the *Mitchells* which succeeded them. The *Lloyd Georges* and *Norfolk Giants* were diseased as was the variety of *St Walfried*, which I believe originated in Holland. I found when I came home after the War that we had a field of *St Walfrieds* at the Gothens. In that field the picking was a race against time. We had to get off as much of the fruit as we could before the fruiting canes died which they usually did well before the end of the season.

In 1953, the Government set up a new research station to help the soft-fruit industry. The Scottish Horticultural Research Institute [SHRI] was established at Mylnefield on the outskirts of Dundee and took over the work started by Dr Cadman and Dr Wood who were both appointed to the staff of the Institute. Dr Cadman had introduced a virus-free stock of *Lloyd Georges* from New Zealand and newer and better stocks of raspberry plants were coming forward from East Malling and now also from the plant breeding section at Mylnefield.

In the early days of the SHRI the scientists tended to keep themselves to themselves. Growers, or so we felt at the time, were regarded as untouchables. Relations got so bad that eventually a meeting was held in Dundee in which members of the Mylnefield staff spent an unpleasant evening listening to the vociferous complaints of the growers' representatives that they got no help and no information about what the research station was trying to do. I must confess that I rather enjoyed the meeting. My only regret was that most of the staff members put up on the platform to answer our complaints were not those responsible for the way in which the station was being run.

Fortunately, there were changes in the institute a short time later. Dr Colin Cadman became Director and for the remainder of its life as a Horticultural Institute, Mylnefield was of a very great value to Scottish growers, not only for the propagation of new raspberry varieties, but also as a place were scientists and the ordinary grower could meet and exchange views for the benefit, I think, of both. Unfortunately, there have been further changes and this time, in my opinion, for the worse. The SHRI and the Scottish Plant Breeding Station amalgamated as an economy measure in 1981 and I am rather afraid that, in its new form, it may not be able to continue to provide the same amount of benefit to the soft fruit industry.

Between the wars we used to have over 800 pickers accommodated at the Gothens each season. For a year or two afterwards there was not too much difficulty in getting pickers, but we had other troubles. In 1948, the first year when pre-emption of the crop by the Government was discontinued, there seemed every chance of a good crop. We had a biggish acreage and I expected around 200 tons. At the start of the third week in May I sold at the high price then ruling. We had heavy frosts a few days later on the nights of 23, 24 and 25 May. When I walked round the fields afterwards, I could not find a single green bud. Every bud I broke was blackened by frost. Things might have been worse. Fortunately for me, I had sold my whole crop, tonnage unspecified and not the actual tonnage I expected to have at the date of sale, otherwise I might have been liable for large damages for breach of contract. In fact, second laterals did grow on many of the bushes and we eventually picked a late crop of over 100 tons.

Our next difficulty in the days of full employment was a shortage of pickers. It was very difficult to find enough of them to get all the fruit picked and this position, strangely enough, still applies in the present times of mass unemployment. As well as accommodating pickers at the farm, we had to bring them in by bus. The weather is an even worse problem than usual when pickers came by bus. A wet morning means no pickers. An early shower and they are away home with nobody left to pick if the sun shines in the afternoon. There are other problems too. The gang bosses will send their squads wherever the crop is the best or their commission highest.

About twenty years ago one of my gang bosses from Fife had missed me out for several days and I could get no reply from his phone. I guessed I might have difficulty in finding him, so I went to Newburgh that night with a letter in my pocket telling him that if he forgot to send me pickers, I'd forget to pay the balance I still owed him and sue him for breach of contract as well. I hammered at the door of his house and, after some scuffling noises, the door opened slightly. His wife told me he was at a garage on the other side of the village and I'd find him there. I left the letter with her and tried the garage and, of course, there was no sign of him. When I got back to his house, he was at the door with my letter in his hand. He told me that I was a hard, unjust man. He had, he said, spoken to his son that very afternoon and arranged for his son's bus to bring me a big load the next day. A few hours after I got back to the farm, he phoned me and, without any sign of embarrassment, he asked me to meet his son's bus at the top of Beech Hedges the next morning at 7.30 and divert it to the Gothens instead of to Cransley where it had been sent.

In the early 50s, I read in an American magazine that a mechanical picker was being used in the state of Washington. With the help of Mr Will Grant of Bissets I tried out three prototypes, but none of them worked. I was then told that the American machine too had been a failure, but some ten years later, I heard that machines were working well in Oregon. The hibernating bee in my bonnet started buzzing furiously once again and I became a one-man pressure group trying to persuade the Department of Agriculture to investigate machine harvesting. The SHRI at Mylnefield was interested and very helpful, but could do nothing without Government approval. Eventually in 1966 a delegation of scientists and growers went to America to see the various machines at work and produced a report recommending that one of the harvesters produced by Agriculture Sciences Inc. of Portland, Oregon should be purchased for trials in Scotland.

For several years afterwards, little was done to implement this recommendation but, with a little financial help from some of the larger growers, Barclay Ross & Hutchison of Aberdeen became interested and produced a harvester that did quite good work. Mr Bill Hally of Alyth, working quite separately, also made a machine which showed considerable promise. Later on an Agriculture Sciences Harvester was imported and used for extensive trials at Mylnefield and elsewhere. The Pattenden Engineering Company from Kent then produced a machine apparently based on the Agriculture Sciences Harvester, but incorporating valuable improvements made by Allan Ramsay formerly of the NIAE [National Institute of Agricultural Engineering] Scotland. A Pattenden Harvester owned by Stewart Farms Ltd is used during the season on raspberry fields at Pittendreich, Meikleour. There are still some difficulties about reliability and our varieties are not so easy to harvest mechanically as those in the USA, but I am sure that, in a few years time, we will have a machine which can be used to get off at least the jamming berries and supplement the hand pickers who will still be needed to pick the real quality fruit.

Now, in 1987, I think the largest grower in the area and also one of the biggest fruit merchants is Sandy Inverarity. Other large scale growers are the Stewart family, the Thomsons and Messrs Neil, Redford, Tanner and Frampton and the CWS [Co-operative Wholesale Society].

The 1986 statistics show that Scotland had 5500 acres under raspberries last year. This is a considerable reduction from the acreage of the seventies but, due to modern high yielding varieties, mainly *Glen Clova* from Mylnefield, the yield of 12,000–13,000 tonnes is roughly the same. This, then is the story of the growth of an industry. From a total of three or four acres in the early 1890s, to tens of acres by the turn of the century, to hundreds of acres when Essendy and Aberuthven came into bearing and, later, to the thousands of acres we have today.

6

LIFE AWAY FROM HOME

Seasonal dwellings, from the hastily constructed bivouacs which leave little or no trace to the 'city' that was Essendy, usually only appear in the historical record in connection with recording innovations or reporting on shortcomings. In this chapter we will hear also from some of those who provided accommodation for seasonal workers and from those who were themselves seasonal dwellers. When viewed across time and space these dwellings can tell us about the ebb and flow of rural life and the industries that thrived, and faded, outside our cities, towns and villages.

In the first decade of the twentieth century housing for migratory and seasonal workers came under the spotlight of a Royal Commission investigation and subsequent report.[136] This work considered a diverse range of workers that included berry pickers, herring gutters, navvies, potato diggers and Travellers. The general conclusion, which was not positive, alluded to the negligence at that time being not much less obvious than at the beginning of the nineteenth century. In the detail, however, some areas fared better and this included the fruit pickers' accommodation in parts of Perthshire which the Commission, members of which had visited Essendy, regarded as provision that catered well for the berry pickers who stayed there.

The local Sanitary Inspector for Blairgowrie, Robert McNicoll, who gave evidence to the Commission, referred to a police census in 1905 which found there to be about 4273 persons picking fruit in the area of the burgh.[137] Surveys like this one, although perhaps not entirely accurate, do provide information which it would be difficult to find anywhere else. Of the 4273 cited in this report, 2000 pickers were identified as locals, a further 1400 were housed by growers and an estimated 100 stayed in common lodging-houses in Blairgowrie. The remaining number would have stayed in shelters such as outhouses, tents or, in the words of the Inspector's statement, 'kraals'.[138] Others still would have simply slept rough in the local woodlands or under any other suitable cover. Near the berry dreels it was commonplace to find families by the riverside camping under coverings of every conceivable kind which included bits of canvas, old bags and pieces of linoleum. Although such conditions may seem harsh in the extreme, it is nonetheless important to remember that, for the poorest at least, urban housing at that time was also challenging, often over-crowded and extremely meagre.

Compared to the alternatives, the accommodation at Essendy in its early days was extremely commodious. The Essendy blocks were on a beautiful site about three miles out of town, on a level platform looking towards the valley of Stormont and the Atholl hills in the distance. The buildings were made of brick with corru-gated iron roofs: hence the nickname, the tin city. The complex formed a quadrangle and as well as the dormitories housed kitchens, stores and meeting halls, a post office and telephone box. The buildings had been erected at considerable expense by the growers; a collective which included masons, joiners, tailors, lawyers, clergymen, a grocer's widow, a social worker and a bar-man. The scheme was administered by local solicitors, Keay & Hodge, who initially had control of the large estate. The syndicate subsequently bought the Essendy Estate, which comprised 450 acres, in 1902. Of this, 200 acres were sold to a neighbouring proprietor and the rest was subdivided into smallholdings of five to forty acres. The motivation behind the development of Essendy is made clear by the growers who wanted, in the language of the day, to get rid of 'tramp labour and replace them with respectable pickers'.[139]

Figures show that 400 women (and girls over 13) from good backgrounds were recruited as a result of this initiative. This included fifty women from The Scottish Council for Women's Trades and eighty from the Salvation Army. In 1906 the female pickers at the Essendy camp were expected to be of a high standard of character and conduct and were required to provide written references from a clergyman, employer or other responsible person before they could start work at the berries.

300 boys from two industrial schools were also enlisted, although they were perceived to be less than able pickers. However, the evidence shows that they did do very well and picked nearly 100 tons in a month, for £482 in wages.[140] Some of the girls were extremely good pickers and the best of them could earn in excess of £2–£3 for three weeks work. In J. M. Hodge's book, *Raspberry Growing in Scotland*, there is a photograph of industrial school children marching to Essendy preceded by their brass band. In accordance with the ethos of the school governors the troubled, and often troublesome, children were to be provided with good wholesome food and basic literacy and numeracy skills while being trained in industrial habits of labour and general usefulness. For the industrial school boys Friday afternoon and Saturday evening were given over to recreation with provision for a range of sporting pursuits as well as concerts in the dining hall. The boys also attended a separate religious service on Saturday, while local ministers and the Salvation Army provided spiritual enlightenment both in the hall and out of doors.

Accommodating so many workers required a huge level of organisation and the evidence for this is impressive. Two kitchens at Essendy catered for three spacious dining rooms which together served 1000 pickers. Outside dining times, one of the dining halls was used as a writing room and another, which contained a piano, served as a recreation space. Strict temperance rules applied. Each of the 48 dormitories on the development held twenty pickers who were accommodated on durable iron beds. Drying sheds and lavatories were adjoining. Essendy was essentially a self-contained community. On-site staff included a medical officer, policeman and a cleansing officer. It is testimony to the way Essendy was run that in 14 years no epidemic or outbreak of serious illness was reported. The accommodation was run along co-operative lines. Each grower had a *pro indiviso* interest in the buildings and this was worked out according to their proportionate acreage: the development was unique in the UK at that time.

Pickers could cook their own food or eat in the canteen. The plain simple diet provided in the dining hall included:[141]

Meat or mince and potatoes	3d
Soup	1d
Pudding	1d
Ham sandwich	1–2d
Porridge with milk	1½d
Tea or cocoa, per cup	½d
Bread and butter, per slice	½–1d
Plate of cold boiled ham	2d

A list of items and prices for the farm shop in 1950 provides an interesting snapshot regarding diet, price and the choice available:

Wrapped bread	6 d loaf
Scones	1d each
Pies	4d and 4½d
Fairy cakes	2½d each
Cheese	…
Bacon	…

Jam	from 1/4½ per lb jar
Beans	10½d per tin
Spaghetti	6½d and 10d per tin
Tomato soup	1/3d per tin
Kippered herring	1/2d per tin
Fish cakes	1/-
Potted meat	11d
soap	6d per ½ bar
boot polish	4½d per tin
luncheon meat	2/9d per tin
rhubarb	1/3d
tomato sauce	1/6½d large bottle
milk	9d and 1/3d per tin
herrings in sauce	1/4d

The beds provided were for two and this reflected the practice of many of the female pickers who went to the berries with companions or as part of a group. Comfortable bedding was also provided and the toilet facilities included the provision of basins, boot brushes and mirrors. There was also separate accommodation for washing and drying clothes.

Gothens, which was three miles outside of Blairgowrie and home to and owned by the Hodge family was one of the larger farms. In 1937 the outside female dormitories at Gothens were reduced from 32 to fewer than 16 and those pickers who attended in 1936 were subsequently given first option to take up the best accommodation on offer the following year.

Andrew Hodge believed there would have been several hundred pickers on the farm between the wars. Recalling his own childhood memories, he told me:

Andrew Hodge (b.1958)
When I was a boy, in the 1960s, I think that figure would be nearer [150–200] … housed as families in the dormitories.
And where were the bulk of the pickers from?
In those days, without doubt, Glasgow.

Of the facilities for pickers at Gothens home farm, he recalled:

Andrew Hodge (b.1958)
The dormitories were exceedingly primitive. I think there were earth floors, bunks, mattresses that were straw-filled sacks, so they must have been extremely itchy. But it was the summer months, late June, July to September. People smoked. There must have been health and safety concerns … I mean people smoked all the time, so potentially there could have been a fire and a serious loss of life. But yes, I am aware of the County Council taking an interest in sanitation, drains and water, and I remember electricity going into the dormitories, which was considered by [my father] to be a terrible expense just for six weeks' work. And, I also remember an inspector coming out from the Council to have a look without my father's permission. And I remember my father meeting this gentleman, and [my father] gave him a severe dressing down.

Mrs Margaret Miller and her husband lived at Gothens for twenty-five years. In his role as grieve, Mr Miller was in charge of five full-time men on the farm. They kept a few hens for eggs and tended a small vegetable garden. Of the pickers she recalled:

Margaret Miller (1931–2014)
They would come about the Glasgow Fair … and the huts where they stayed were just down the road, quite near to the house. It was quite an eye-opener in a way, but it was how they

settled in. It just became a way of life there.

… at that time they had to go to Blairgowrie for all their shopping. The Co-operative van came round twice a week, but very often they were out picking when the van came round.

Mrs Miller eventually started up a small shop of her own, selling lemonade and crisps, sweets and suchlike.

Like the herring gutters who lived in basic huts when following the fishing in the Northern Isles, attempts were made by some of the berry pickers to transform their sheds into something more homely. Andrew Hodge remembered that workers who returned year on year would often leave belongings in storage at Gothens. Colourful covers were brought along for the bunk beds as well as rugs for the floor: in this way one supposes the austerity of camp life was made more homely.[142]

Close comparisons can be made with other forms of seasonal dwelling in other parts of the UK and George Orwell's literary account of life on the hop-picking farms of Kent provides a comparative example. Just as at Gothens, huts were set aside each year for the best pickers and families. The hop pickers often came from London's east end and, as this oral history extract shows, they too would domesticise their huts for the season:

Mrs D___, London (b.1929)
You used to get your hut … . But oh! they was like sheds! Stables are better. Take the odd rolls of wallpaper and stick them up. Or a bit of, well, it used to be distemper in them days. You'd fill a couple of bed ticks with straw and sew 'em up … . Yeh, you'd use the tea chests, that you took your gear in, for a table. Pots and pans and me bit of china. Take that home and bring it down when we went. A few lace curtains. Used to take a bit of lace curtain to put round the door and round me bed. Make it like a four poster. Old bit of mat down.[143]

To return to Gothens, Margaret Miller shared these memories of the pickers:

Margaret Miller (1931–2014)
Big families some o them. One of the biggest was the McCulleys. They had a big family and 'old grannie' as we called her. She wis just a tiny little wizened woman. She looked efter the hut, tidied, [made] the meals. And the first thing she did whenever they came through from Glasgow, she made them all sweep out the hut and clean it all out before they moved their stuff in.
Do you know what parts of Glasgow they tended to come from?
I can't just remember where they came from, but some came from the multis. But you got to know them and, of course, there was a register kept and it was most of the same ones that came back every year. They were well warned. If there was trouble, they were out. They didn't get back and their names were taken off the register. But I think we'd only one family that didn't get back …

It was a culture shock to me in a way, but it was amazing just how much you got to enjoy them and miss them after they went for a while. We used to enjoy the hustle and bustle …

I was never 'Mrs Miller', it was always 'Mrs Wallace' and 'Mr Wallace'. Wallace was my husband's first name. I always remember, one time we were coming back from Glasgow Central. My second son had just had his posting out at Plymouth, in the Navy, and we were all coming home. Of course, we had to change trains at Glasgow and all of a sudden we heard these voices shouting: 'Hello, Mr Wallace. Hello!' Oh, my goodness, here were the young berry pickers, in the middle of Glasgow Central station. It was hilarious.

Margaret Miller described the huts from her time as being 'basic' with best of straw palliasses and a separate building with a hotplate where cooking could be done. By this time, the numbers coming for the fair fortnight were reduced to about fifty or sixty. For the majority who did make the journey from Glasgow, coming to the berries was by then primarily an opportunity for a holiday in the country. As one lady recalled by Margaret said, 'We've had a holiday and I've got five pounds left out [of] the berry money and I'm happy as Larry'.

Into the 1980s some diehards among the Glaswegian exodus were still coming to stay at the Blairgowrie berry farms, or in huts or sheds outside the town. They shared toilets, a single shower and washing facilities and a communal kitchen which might have had a log-fired range and a couple of calor gas burners. This last item was a mod con. The huts were made of wood with tarry felt roofs with plasterboard partitions which afforded little privacy. But it would have become a home from home while they were there. Large families still came each summer, working for up to a rate of twelve pence per kilo. Additionally, in contrast to the English fruit farms which were 'pick your own' by this time, hundreds of pickers still continued to be bussed in daily to the Scottish soft fruit farms.

Away from Blairgowrie and the fruit farms we can explore an assortment of other temporary dwellings associated with seasonal occupations.

The Irish workers who came to mainland Britain in huge numbers in the late nineteenth and early twentieth century were another significant group of migrant workers who sought a temporary home. And they came in huge numbers. In 1892, for example, 17,607 harvest tickets were issued from County Mayo railway stations for men and women travelling between early March and the end of November.[144] They came to plant potatoes, for turnip work, harvesting and general farm work. Most of those who made the journey were from west Mayo, especially Achill,[145] and west Donegal.[146]

Migrant workers from Mayo, Donegal and Galway who travel-led to Scotland came in squads of between twenty to thirty people and the accommodation for them has been thoughtfully explored by Heather Holmes.[147] The Scottish potato merchants, who bought the crop from the farmer while it was still in the ground, often also provided sufficient bedding, fuel and lighting for their squads while transport and work arrangements were left to the local gaffer or ganger. As required, the gangers would also often make additional trips to Ireland, to areas such as north Donegal, to recruit additional pickers. Those from Arranmore were often strongly bound by close kinship ties, increasing the solidarity within the squad, so there would be differences in the accepted protocol of hiring and dispersal once the groups of pickers arrived in Scotland.[148]

When I caught up with respected Perthshire farmer, James McLaren, outside Crieff in the mid-1980s he told me what he remembered about the Irish squads:

James McLaren (b.1912)
Now on the subject of labour – not the men who were fee'd but seasonal labour – can you recall whether Irish workers were ever taken on in this part of Perthshire?
Oh yes, very much so. Muthill was quite an Irishman's strong-hold because James Haggart, the local potato merchant at that time, grew a lot of potatoes. And, of course, potatoes are still a lot o work but they were even more work then when they were mostly worked by hand. James Haggart brought over a great number of Irish to this area. Some were only seasonal, but a great many o them stayed on all year at the Haggart's buildings at the top of Muthill – which are away now. Those buildings were filled with Irish and you wouldn't believe the number of people.

When we had a bothy at Fintloch, a two-room bothy with no toilet facilities, I've known 16 people living in it, men and women. And there was nobody to complain or say why shouldn't they do it; and they carried their water from a tap outside and used a privy outside as well. But they lived in very confined spaces.

The Housing (Scotland) Act, 1925 gave local authorities power to make by-laws for housing seasonal workers, however Anne O'Dowd rightly remarks that this did not necessarily mean the local authorities made use of this power, or that all the premises were inspected annually'.[149] James McLaren's memories certainly support this assertion.

Author, Patrick MacGill, was born in west Donegal and had direct experience of migrant work and living conditions. He describes this in his books and his observations are valuable in telling us about the peripatetic way of life as he experienced it in the early twentieth century. From his days of grinding childhood poverty as one of a family of eleven, McGill's preparation for a literary life was the very antithesis of Irish contemporaries such as Yeats or Joyce.

On my bicycle odyssey across Scotland in September 1984, a farmer very kindly gave me free use of one of his cottages for the weekend. Situated at the foot of Glen Lethnot, it had been recently vacated by tattie roguers. I had been warned it was 'basic' but the promise of a roof over my head was enough for me to seize the opportunity. A mustard-coloured door led to the toilet, which was as warm as a snow hole. The sitting room was furnished with sticks of furniture and there was a long sofa and an old TV at one side. The TV didn't work, nor did the fridge. My tea that night was a cold smokie and a glass of water. The only light was provided by a single candle. When I turned in for the night and blew out the candle the pinhead of light from the wick seemed to last ages before it disappeared. A new day brought ice-cold water to wash in followed by the unexpected but very welcome surprise of a full fry-up down at the farm. Such kindness is not forgotten and remains still in my memory. That night I had slept well, stretched out on the sofa in my three-season sleeping bag, but the experience certainly gave me an insight into the living conditions endured by the tattie workers.

The humble bicycle has played an important part in the history of seasonal rural employment and we have already heard about this in relation to Blairgowrie and the berry workers. Mass-production brought the bicycle within reach of the pockets of many and it is no exaggeration to state that for many working men and women in the country it was the bicycle that expanded their horizons, for both work and social activities.

Speaking in a broad Angus or 'Forfarshire' brogue former bothy-loon Joe Tindal explained the importance of a bike for his own social life:

Joe Tindal (b.1916, Kirkton of Monikie, Angus)
… If ye wanted tae gae onieplace it wis a case o jist jump oan yer bike an go. Ach, Ah've biked for miles tae gae tae a dance. Ah've biked fae Ladenfaird [Ladenford] up tae Lintrathen, fae Ladenfaird tae Carnoustie on a Saturday nicht tae gae tae the dancin.
What sort o mileage?
Ah well, that wid be twenty, 26 mile – that again.
Can ye mind yer first bike?
Ma first bike wis a Royal Enfield an Ah peyed five pound ten fir it. An Ah didna get a help fae oniebuddy. Hed tae buy it masel. Ye jist hed tae ging an gie the man ten boab at a time, mibbe oan a Seterday, an this payed fer yer bike … . It wis a lad, Hill, in Farfar [Forfar] that Ah bocht ma first bike fae, an Ah hid it fer years an years.
Did ye hae a carbide lamp?
Ah did that. An Ah got stoppit wi the police fer it no been burnin!

Joe Tindal recalled biking at weekends from his parent's house at the Mains of Brigton to a bothy at Seaside of Errol, in the Carse of Gowrie (about thirty miles away). Later, after he was married, he would regularly cycle to Dundee, to Bell's Fair, which was where men could be fee'd on the first Friday in October.

Single farm workers were often housed in bothies. Before Andrew Bruce migrated south from Aberdeenshire to Angus and Perthshire, he worked at farms including the six-pair farm of Little Lour and the four-pair farm at Fletcherfield. He could recall being in bothies where some of the older men still used wooden brose bowls and horn spoons to sup with. Andrew, who was born in Inverurie, shared with me some of his memories of the bothy culture which prevailed in Aberdeenshire:

Andrew Bruce (b.1913)
They were different up in Aberdeenshire again. They got their meals in the hoose. Thir wis naebody fed thirsels. The accommodation at a lot of the big places wis caad the chaumer, an it wis often above stable in big loft, ye ken, partitioned off, wae the beds in there.

The exception to eating in the farmhouse was Sunday breakfast:

Andrew Bruce (b.1913)
The horse lads taen shot aboot buyin sassages. Noo say there wis six, well we'd o haen tae buy three pund o sassages an ye'd aboot five sassages each. That wis aboot ten or something in a pund in those days an ye ay bocht guid sassages for aboot echtpence or ninepence a pund. Noo ye hed them on a Sunday mornin an if ye managed tae pick up an egg in the manger or in the stall, ye could o stuck it in wae it tae.

The bothy lads had a rota, known as pannie, for doing chores:

Joe Tindal (b.1916)

Aye, fer hackin sticks. Ye had a week hackin sticks; everybuddy
taen a week at the sticks. If you [were in] the bothy an didna hae
tae go oot an sort horse, you made the porridge, an tea in the
mornin for the men comin in. Then if thir wis ony porridge left,
this wis kept till dennertime an ye had cald porridge – calders.
That must o been gey rough?
No, ye thocht nothin aboot it … . Ye could hae calders ae day
an mibbe the next day ye wid hae brose at nicht cos this wis nae
fry-ups in a bothy at that time. The only time the fryin pan wis
oan in a bothy wis a Sunday mornin.

There were various types of oatmeal-based options but the diet
was, in the main, unrelenting and monotonous and luxuries such
as cooked meat were absent:

Joe Tindal (b.1916)

The porridge was made in a muckle three-leggit pot that hung
fae a swey ower the fire. Thir wis sae muckle porridge it took a
lang time tae cuil, so whiles it wis pit oot the bothy door tae sit
a whiley.

Andrew Bruce said that, in his experience, brose was on the
way out by the early 1930s. This impression was reiterated by Joe
Tindal:

Joe Tindal (b.1916)

Och, they died out gradually jist when things began tae change
over. An that wis anither law o the bothy. See yer bowl – ye
derennae wash that bowl. If you gaed hame at May month, that
bowl wisna washed until November. If ye washed it ye hed tae
ging an buy anither een. The boys jist taen it an broke it. Aye…
thir wis some awfie funny things in the bothy … . Ye sat wae yer

18. Patrick Hodge and Martin Doherty, 1968.
The dormitories can be seen in the background.

Courtesy of Hodge Archive

19. Weigh station, 1968. Left to right: John Hodge (at cash box),
weighman Martin Doherty (beside scales) and Tommy Gilmartin (gang
boss, Newbridge, Fife). A young boy at the back is stacking empty pails.

Courtesy of Hodge Archive

20. Small group of pickers at North Corston Farm. The pail strapped to the picker's waist was known as a luggie and the contents would be tipped into larger buckets for weighing.

Courtesy of Joan Kettles

21 and 22 Auchen Campbell worked at Gothens Farm for over forty years and retired to a cottage on the farm. His real name was Dudley but he was given the name by his co-workers as he came from Auchenblae and Dudley was considered too posh a name for a farm worker. His wife, Mary Bryce, came over from Ireland to pick potatoes and she is seen here wearing a wrap-over pinafore similar to those often worn by pickers. Mary is pictured at Carsie Bridge Cottages.[194]

Courtesy of Hodge Archive

23. Raspberry pickers, possibly at Blairgowrie,
early twentieth century.

Image © National Museums Scotland

24 and **25.** J. M. Hodge.

Above: Hodge on a trap,
on a ranch in Canada
which he bought on behalf
of a syndicate *c.*1908.

Left: Hodge doing a BBC
radio broadcast from
Gothens Farm, mid-1930s.

Courtesy of Hodge Archive

26. Moor Field at Gothens, Second World War. D. Wilson Laing (standing).

Courtesy of Hodge Archive

27. G. M. Hodge, beside a mechanical harvester, Oregon, July 1966. G. M. Hodge was instrumental in encouraging innovation in soft-fruit production.

Courtesy of Hodge Archive

28. Tents beside the raspberry fields, near Blairgowrie, 1957.

Image © National Museums Scotland

29. Letter confirming the appointment of Wallace Miller
     to the post of grieve at Gothens Farm.

30. Wallace and Margaret Miller.   31. Wallace Miller.

Courtesy of Margaret Gordon, daughter of Wallace and Margaret

32. Aerial shot of Gothens, *c.*1958. Andrew Hodge provided this information: In front of the steading there appears to be a storage area for barrels. This is where they were washed. Also visible in the stackyard, above a haystack, are what appear to be 3 cwt casks which were used when the fruit market was weak and fruit had to be held back and preserved. The area of concrete on the right of the house was the site of the shop. Dormitories were also located nearby. These were moved to nearer the A93 when the family moved into the farmhouse, *c.*1956.

Courtesy of Hodge Archive

33. Gothens staff, probably from the canteen, 1943.
Courtesy of Hodge Archive

34. Berry machine harvesting the crop by going along each side of the dreel and shaking the raspberries off the bushes. The umbrella on top provided shade from the summer sun for Audrey and John Kettles, *c.*1996.

Courtesy of
Joan Kettles

35. Audrey Kettles removing bad fruit, leaves and any other foreign materials as the berries pass through the mechanised harvester, 1996.

Courtesy of
Joan Kettles

36. Hawkhill, Dundee, looking east, 1964.

Old Dundee Photo Album. Turner Mckinlay Collection,
Courtesy of University of Dundee Archive: Ref: CMS 4/1/16 (21)

37. Pea buster stall as recalled by Bernadette Dailly

Courtesy of Dundee Libraries, Leisure and Culture B07.035

bowl an ye could get the finger marks richt roond yer bowl. Yer bowl wis pitten intae yer meal kist – nivver washed. Ye taen yer tea oot o the bowl tae. Aathing wis taen oot o yer bowl.

The bothies or lodges of the Tay salmon netsmen were equally austere, especially at the start of the season in the early spring when the cold temperature was an important factor. In the 1980s I was given a glimpse of just how difficult this way of life could be when I interviewed Tom Jarvis Jnr:

Tom Jarvis Jnr (b. 1936)

I've heard ma wife's father talkin about the Abernethy fishing station in the 20s. Their bothy was on Mugdrum Island and there was no way they could get rid o the rats because Mugdrum Island was infested with rats at that time. He's wakened up in the morning and counted over forty running about the floor of the bothy. It was riddled with holes. You see it was just the earth floor into the bank o the river. They blocked up one hole and ten minutes later there was another one burrowed through. All their foodstuffs had to be kept in glass jars, and even when they were sitting eating, there was often a rat would jump up on the table to get to the food.

Local Carse of Gowrie historian, Lawrence Melville, writing in 1939 of the bothies of fifty years before was certainly not too far off the mark by referring to them as 'dens' that were excavated into the side of the river.[150] The insanitary conditions of the Tay and Earn bothies were raised in the House of Commons after the inspector, Alexander Carmichael, prepared a report for the Board of Supervision after inspecting more than fifty lodges in April 1889. The lodges housed up to seven men and were rightly condemned on a number of counts: insufficient air space, inadequate ventilation, earth flooring, lack of privvies, inadequate storage space and rubbish dumping nearby.[151] Over the years the lodges underwent change and refurbishment but, as Tom Jarvis Jnr has explained, the earlier lodges had left an indelible impression on the men who lived in them.

Conditions in the netsmen's lodges were never uniform and individual experiences often depended upon which part of the Tay or Earn crews were fishing. Certain lodges were double-crewed, which meant each shift was swapping over with another dictated by the tide times. In these lodges at least the crew coming off would be hopping into a warm bed which had only recently been vacated by his opposite shift partner.

It was harsh and completely without domesticity:

> **Tom Logie (b.1904)**
> There was no table or nothin. You brocht a fish box in and there was a big kettle set on the fireside ready; one of these gunmetal lads, an the water was always burning. And maybe an hour or so gaun on shift time again, you got up and it was always ham and egg … or sausage and egg, or something like that. But there were no tinned meat in those days. Ye got nothin like that.

> **John Scobie (b.1920)**
> You washed in the burn at the side o the bothy [and] thir wisnae any motor transport or motor cobles then. It was the pushbike or walk. Ye cycled down five miles maybe, down through the fields, an that is how ye got down to the waterside. The ropey [youngest] – that was me – always usetae get away early to have the kettle boiled before the other ones finished, or maybe the fryin pan heated.

John Barrie, a Newburgh man, could recall, from his days as a gaffer with the Tay Salmon Fisheries Company, that in the lower reaches of the Tay the bothies had the old-fashioned double beds and the men slept in twos:

John Barrie (b.1912)
You went out and got the water from springs. If you wanted a toilet you had to go round the back o the bothy intae the wood. But we'd bits o good fun at that time. You made yer ain fun. It wisnae an unusual thing for some o your opposite crews gaun climbin up on the bloody roof an puttin a wet bag over the bloody chimney: that wis good fun. One thing you were never short o was coal. By God, they kept you wae a plentiful supply o coal … . They'd load up a coble wae maybe a ton and a half, an took it doon tae yer bothy.

Jim Davidson, a joiner and boat-builder who was also based in Newburgh, gave this description of the bothies which, he recalled, measured roughly 30 x 15 feet:

Jim Davidson (b.1934)
There wis only one door and that normally faced the water, with a window on each side of the door. Once you were in the door, the dividing wall ran from the door to the back wall, with a big coal fire on each side of the dividing wall … a stone floor and a couple of wooden tables to eat off, and benches – form seats … . All the cooking utensils you had was one great big black kettle, and maybe a pan or two which you used for cooking.

Here, Jim and the other informants are describing the older generation of lodges on the Fife side of the River Tay. I visited some of these, such as Lower Tay Lodge, on fieldwork trips in the mid-1980s. They stood alongside evidence of earlier dwellings and it looked likely that some stones from the earlier bothies were re-used for the later dwellings. The masonwork was accomplished and impressive. Stone and dressed sandstone quoins were evident and the symmetry of the floor plan and elevations along classical lines indicated that these had been built from a pattern book. Inside were some of the old iron bedsteads: a reminder of the crews who had last fished and lived in these riverside dwellings. In some, the salmon-pink distemper was fading from the wall on a plaster base. Patches of lathwork were exposed from the ceiling and the graffiti of interlopers provided evidence of more recent occupation.

Based in these Fife bothies it was possible, in later years, for the men to meet mobile shops at the top of the road to buy supplies which would have included bacon, eggs, cheese, bridies, pies, sausages, bread and tinned meats.

For the netsmen who had migrated south from the Outer Hebrides any efforts for a social life were confined to within the bothy. After the hard physical shifts there would have been little time or energy left but they did make their own music, as Scalpay-born Angus Morrison reflected:

Angus Morrison (1925–2008)

When we arrived in Perth, the Tay Salmon Fisheries lorry met us at the railway station and I was taken, along with the rest of the people from Scalpay, north to the Tay. The mattress was a straw mattress – that was supplied – and this big black kettle. That, I think, was all that was waiting for us in the bothy … . We not only slept there, we lived there as well. There was no other place for us to go. I would say it was adequate. We had another set of Scalpay lads next door, and one of these lads had a button-key accordion … so from time to time we had our moments there too.

As with the farm bothies, music was an important form of

recreation and many a Scottish dance band musician must surely have started out here. Books were unknown and newspapers, if you were lucky, might include titles such as the *People's Journal* or the *Weekly News*, but the gloomy conditions would not have encouraged much reading. In the lighter summer evenings, and when energy levels allowed, the workers might enjoy sports or trials of strength, such as the sweir tree or shot put. Throwing the hammer and quoits (using the muckle shoes of Clydesdale horses) were also popular.

Given the physical nature of farm work I asked Jim Ogg about any particular memories he had about local strong men:

> **Jim Ogg (b.1906)**
> Oh aye. Dave Stewart, he wis reckoned tae be a very strong boy. He'd tak a bag o corn an just throw it up oan his back like that, nae bother tae him: twelve stone [in weight] … . Some o them ye'd tae tak wae a pinch o salt, ye ken. They'd say 'Oh so-an-so usetae pull a cairt, an somebody lifted a hoarse', an onything like that. Believe it if ye like …
>
> Auld Geordie Ferrier usetae lift a hoarse off the grund. He crawled in ablow his belly an rose up, an the horse's feet [lifted] up off the grund. Geordie Robb wis a stong lad. He wid tak a cairt exle an twa o us sittin oan the end an the wheels oan it an lift it half aff the grund … Ah'm tellin ye … Ah've seen him daen it.

As the Kent hop pickers had their tea chests, so the single lads had their kists, as Jim Ogg recalled from his own experiences of flitting time:

> **Jim Ogg (b.1906)**
> Whenever they wir leavin they geyed tae the fermer they wir goin tae an they got a horse and cairt there. They [then] cam

for their kist an took it away fae the farm. The[y] jist had a single kist, some hud a box jest, no a kist ata, an ah thir goods wis packed intae that … . [The] only time Ah hud ma name oan ma kist wis when Ah left Portlaggie an gaed tae Ardgamelaw an pit [ma kist] oan the train at the Brig o Earn tae Perth Station. Ah think it cost ye thruppence or somethin. *Going back tae the 1920s, what would a single lad in a bothy hev inside his kist for the six month?*
Inside it! He'd mibbe hae a suit o claes an his shirts like … . He'd only wan suit o claes an the rest wis ah workin claes, and they wir generally hingin up about the bothy aa the time. Then ye'd anither wee kist, whit we caad a mealer, whaur ye kept yer breid an yer butter an margarine an jam, cheese, an aathing like that. Yer dishes wir never pittin in. They jist ay sat oan the table.

All the time Jim was in the bothies he never saw a clock. It was always a pocket watch hanging from a nail on the bed post 'an ye hud a keek o it in the moarnin tae see if it wis risin time'. This was usually 5.30 am in the summer months, unless the gaffer chapped the men up before that time so as they could prepare their horses.

Like the berry pickers, the bothy dwellers often enjoyed the services of a local mobile shop.[152] When I interviewed mobile shop owner Jock Mollinson, in 1985, he told me about his experiences of working out of Alyth:

Jock Mollinson (b.1908)

In the summertime it wis grand – it wis a hoaliday. In the wintertime it wis hell. Some o the drifts, o fower, five fit high. Fact there wis one year the Kirrie Co-op van – it wis a big, big van – an it wis richt oot o sicht, ye couldnae see it. The only thing ye could see on the top o it wis 'Kirriemuir Equitable Society'. Well, ye didnae go up the glen for three weeks.

Thir wis a brae at Fordwell an ye war up the brae when they wir castin the snaw – they wir castin it richt ooer the tap o the telegraph wires.

Jock went on to describe the challenge of reaching some of the more remote glens in inclement weather:

Jock Mollinson (b.1908)
Oh, rich tae the heid o Glen Isla, richt up at the tap; every farm thir wis, [Ah] went roond them aa. Ye wis lucky if ye got hame, oh ain o clock oan Sunday mornin. Ah tell ye it wis a wild place wis Alyth, a wild place.
Wis this snowbound?
Aye, snowbound – couldnae get doon, power vans couldnae get awa fae Kirkton [of Glenisla]. The richt place tae bide aa the same. Oh it wis grand … . Three times a week we went up tae the glen. Of course, ye'd Lintrathen an that ye'd tae ging tae. That's the next glen … . This is the beginnin o the Second World War. That's when I wis oan it. So I wis a baker tae trade. They wis aa called up an it wis the only wey you could get vanmen. Ye'd a long day o't.

Jock had happy memories of the ploughmen coming in to Alyth to get fee'd at the May or November terms:

Jock Mollinson (b.1908)
Feein day! It wis grand. See aa the ploomen comin in, oh some o them fell … , ken, wae thir tackety buits an ahthing. The brig up the side o the burn oan Commercial Street, this wisnae a railin oan it at that time, an efter the pubs wis shut, by that time they'd be sittin oan the dyke an the feet wid gae awa fae them an ah ye heard wis SPLASH – inta the burn!

Jock's memories remind us again that these temporary dwellings and transient forms of employment created a milieu which was quite unique: so very different to the normal settled existence which many would return to at the end of the season, and which others gravitated towards as the country ways around them were changed by progress.

And we can return to the berryfields for a further evocation of the lives of those who set up temporary homes around Blair during the berry season. When I interviewed Peggie Stewart in 1983, her own memories of camping out next to the berry dreels evoked warm feelings of nostalgia:

Peggie Stewart (b.1925)
Ye wid see them aa sittin an singin round the fire – happy tae. They usetae sing *The Roads Tae Baxter's Mill* and *The Bonnie Woods o Hatton* and *The Berryfields o Blair* … . Oh everything wis happy. Ye ken, Ah think the world's awfie queer noo. Ye don't see the same at aa.[153]

In his evocative short essay on life in the berryfields of Blair, Dr Hamish Henderson captured the spirit of the surroundings in all its verve, vitality and zest for life:

By this time, four or five similar ceilidhs might well be going on in one berry field, and the excited collector … could hear tantalising fragments of a rare 'Child' ballad, or the high flamenco-like cadences of a Gaelic tinker love lament. Recording in the berryfields, in fact was … like holding a tin can under the Niagara Falls; in a single session you can hear everything from ancient Ossianic hero-tales … to the caustic pop song parodies thought up by Clydeside teenagers the same afternoon.[154]

The final words for this chapter come from champion of the Travellers in Scotland, Sheila Stewart. No doubt she was one of those in Hamish's mind when he talked of the berryfields.

Sheila Stewart MBE (1935–2014)
I never learned a song in my life that was written doon. It was aa through the oral tradition because that was the way you had to sing them – the oral tradition with the Travelling people. It's a different way of singing from anybody else because we put the Coinneach in.[155]

Hamish Henderson, and I quote what he said: 'Sheila, there are many branches to a musical tree but the Travelling people are the roots'. And that's to be carried forward … . We had to survive. It was a way of survival at that, and I've been to Princeton and Harvard lecturing about that, and if America's interested in Scottish culture and what we were like going back to the twelfth century, why not Scotland?

7
AT HOME

We return home in this final chapter. Dundonians who had gone to the berries or the tatties, and were interviewed for this study, would often talk about the urban domestic scene they were leaving behind when they left for the countryside each year. Their recollections provide us with valuable contextual information for the working lives described in earlier chapters and can help us to appreciate the living conditions at that time. Themes considered in this chapter include: accommodation and living conditions; the means test; daily chores and routine, food and drink; street life and early working experiences. In terms of locality, predominance is given to memories of the (old) Hawkhill (or 'Hahky' as it is still referred to locally). The reasons for this are two-fold. Firstly, this reflects the quantity of material gathered and acknowledges the impression the Hawkhill has left on the memories of those who lived there. In addition, this tenement area has largely been demolished so the oral history material presented here serves as a marker, adding valuable first-hand accounts to the historical record[156] so that it can be available for future consideration. Hawkhill was once a densely populated area located in west Dundee on the edge of the industrial sector. The area was later developed to make way for expansion by the University of Dundee, the dual carriageway Hawkhill bypass and the creation of brownfield sites for industrial units.[157]

John Jordan (b.1948)

To somebody who wasn't in Hawkhill [and] *Dundee during the 60s, how would you describe it?*

A throng. From the West Port up to Sinderins:[158] shops, pubs, all the different types of shops. There was mens' outfitters, there was meal shops, cycle shops, greengrocer's, fish-n-chip shops. Cabrelli's, opposite Balfour Street, that was one of my favourites as I was pally with the owner's son, Andrew Cabrelli. They lived in Mountpleasant in the university area … . There were cinemas and a dance hall, Robbie's, in the university area that they [used] as an exam hall later on – and that was demolished after that. Down at Temple Lane there was pubs and secondhand shops. In the West Port there was a well-known ironmonger there [and] The Globe Bar, Mickey Coyle's.

Mary Angus (b.1940)

On both sides of the Hawkhill, starting from that lane [Ritchies] up there, every doorway was either a shop or a close. In those days some people stayed in the back shop and there were hundreds of people. Of course, there were the jute mills and [so] you heard the bummers.

Bernadette Dailly (b.1954)

… you'd hear the lorries going up and down. There wasn't a lot of cars. A lot of noise with children and also, you'd hear, if you walked up further, the mills going. … But I remember the bummer would go more when I lived in Lochee, from Cox's. I remember the bummer there, but while in the Hawkhill I don't remember it greatly; maybe just that little bit too young to remember that.

Therese Devlin (b.1957)

There was plenty shops in the Hawkhill. Just across the road from us was the chip shop, a wee grocer's as well, Nicoll's the shoe shop, where we used to go and get our plastic sandals for the summer. I don't remember how long they'd last us but my memory is most likely the straps would get worn and snap. So as you still had somethin to wear, you would cut them and try to make them into flipflops .....

Up the 'Hahky an doon the Blahky' – that's the saying. Dunno where it originated from, but it must o been when folk would go for their Sunday stroll. You'd walk up the Hawkhill and then back down the Blackness Road.[159]

In my memory, wae bein sae young, it wis a very busy place. We stayed in 121A Hawkhill. It was called the frontlands and the backlands. Because once you came through the big close there wis more tenements up the back which came under the Hawkhill as well. And in between was a lot o old air-raid shelters which we played in many, many a time – puttin on shows in a spare bit of ground and everything. My memory is of a busy, friendly place: everybody got on well.

Anne McDonald (b.1946)

There wis tenements, and underneath wis shops, like the pawn shop at the West Port. Above that wis houses in a tenement. The only big houses we ever seen when we were wee was when we went up Blackness Avenue. And when you went up there you knew all the toffs lived there and you'd say, 'When I'm big I'll get ain o thae hooses'. [Laughs] And little did I know that [I'd marry] someone whose auntie lived in Blackness Avenue – and they were schoolteachers – strange, eh? Lovely big houses. But there wis no big houses on the Hawkhill.

Iain Smart (b.1949)

I mean, the Hawkhill was still there when I went in second year [at art college]. We looked at other flats that were garrets, what you'd expect artists to be in. They were in Ure Street and they were going to be knocked down, so you got them to rent dead cheap. There was running water, but that was it, and electricity. *And there was still a community in the Hawkhill?*

Aye. I used to walk down the Hawkhill in [my] first year [there], and there was tenements on both sides, pubs and shops, all the way down to the West Port.

Bernadette and Therese (*née* Mills) came from a large Catholic family of mum, dad and eight children. Their first floor flat in the Hawkhill had a kitchen, living room, three bedrooms and a bathroom with indoor toilet and bath.

Therese Devlin (b.1957)

How unusual was [it to have an indoor toilet]?

Oh, I think it was very unusual. Because we used to run up and down the stairs to the lady that stayed in the attic flat, Mrs James. Because she used to help ma mum looking after us and her toilet was on the outside. It wasn't very nice because she never had toilet paper, it was cut-up newspaper … and she didn't have a bath. [I remember] one time our auntie visited from South Africa [and] we were up stayin at Mrs James and gettin a bath [and] it was actually the old tin bath in front of the fire.

Recalling an earlier era, Peter Taylor remembered:

Peter Taylor (b.1900)

A tap and toilet was out on the stairway and … as regards the rest of the people in the tenement, you often had six families to one small toilet.[160] These 'old maids', as we called them, were always consigned to the attic somehow or other, by the factor. At that time it was all factors. There was no corporation houses.

Living space was at an absolute premium:

Mary Angus (b.1940)
There was six children and my mum and dad: eight of us in two rooms. And Anne will tell you, you used to be standing. And I can't remember sitting, because there was no seats, there wasn't any room … . We had the bed recess as well. We had two beds in the bedroom and the boys were in one … and the girls in the other. And, I think, just a wee wardrobe. And that was all the room we had.

Therese Devlin (b.1957)
About '65 my grandfather took a stroke, ma mum's dad. He had a stroke. So him and his wife came to live with us as well. So between the eight kids, mum and dad, then my gran and grandad, there was twelve of us lived in that three-bedroom flat in the Hawkhill.

Bernadette Dailly (b.1954)
Another memory I've got, when we lived in the Hawkhill, is we had three bedrooms and there was five girls in one bedroom. We'd have two beds, a double and a single, two of us in the single bed and three in the double bed … . Three would go to the bottom and two at the top. I think that was the way it went. … Ah really canna tell you what we used to do, but if it was too cold they'd maybe no get up for the toilet [laughs] because one of the sisters had a problem with her bladder, which is true. Terrible when you think back to these things you did.

Was it typical for folk to hae large families?

It was. When you think of our friends. There was a family
lived in Wilkie's Lane, the McLarens, and there was 14 of them.
That's a family we were quite close with … . They were the first
to get a television, maybe 1960. We were just young and all
went round [there] if something was on the television. We all
sat around this television. Mum and dad and all the family,
with this family of 14, and watched the television. But no, big
families were the norm – it was if you were a Catholic. It would
maybe be a bit different if you weren't, but it was the norm to
have a lot of kids.

Alex Lackie (b.1957)

Meh mum and dad emigrated to America, about 1955. So when
they were in America they had me an Ricky, and they came back
in 1960. The only hoose they could get wis in Broon Street.
There wis six o us lived in a two-bedroom hoose. Yer bath was a
zinc bath. This is 1960, and meant to be the Age of
Enlightenment. Kennedy's comin up to be the President of the
United States and we're livin wae an ootside shitey. This is true
… . It wis an ootside toilet wae a fuckin nail, wae no toilet paper
– [just] newspapers! Ye got a bath wae ether the zinc bath or
sittin in the sink, wan o thae Belfast deep ains.

Recalling his formative years in Lochee, John H. Beaton said:

John H. Beaton MBE (b.1937)

No mains power as such for heating water, for washing clothes,
or for baths – because we didn't have a [proper] bath. We had a
tin bath. My elder brother was the most studious … he would
go in the bath first. There would be water poured in from the
kettle and from pots. He would go in, get washed and get his
hair shampooed. [And] just rinsed with the water still in the

bath, not with fresh clean water. Rinsed the soap away and got rid of most of the debris. Then he would be dried off with a towel. Water would be prepared when he was having his bath. I would then go into the same water, which was still warm, a bit dirty but there was more water to heat up. So I washed and dried myself with the same damp towel. And then the younger brother, who was always the messiest, he would go in for the very same treatment. And then the water would be swilled down this small sink.

Anne McDonald (b.1946)

By that time, the laddies were gettin bigger and we moved up to 22 Bernard Street, and the same [kind of] house …sitting room wae one bedroom. But the room next door wis like a single end as they called it, one big room. My mum got that for the four laddies and Eh got the bedroom to masel. Mum and dad still slept in the kitchen.

What was the level o comfort like in the first ain?

Nothin really. Ah mean it wisnae carpeted like now. There wis a couple o rugs on the floor, lino, naebuddy had carpets: basic really, very basic. Eh mean the sink – ye done everything in that room … . We didna hae a zinc bath. Nope. Maist people washed in the sink to be honest. Everybody did.[161]

Anne Piggott (b.1939)

We lived in Taylor's Lane, one room. It wis like an attic. Five o us in there. No toilet. Nothing. Seven families shared the toilet. Yeah … no runnin water. We got the water at the top of the road.[162]

So how many pots did you commandeer?

Three pots an a kettle … . Sometimes when ma mum went tae the washy Eh went wae her, an she just threw me in the sink [laughs].

Bob Fotheringham (b.1945)

But the stupid thing was, when you finished the Saturday mornin in the jute mill you went to the washhouse. It was then in Guthrie Street,[163] had yer bath, and ye went [home] with your working clothes, went home and put your good clothes on. [laughs] Stupid. But oh, it wis great!

What was the atmosphere like in the washy?

Oh, it wis good if ye got somebody in who wis a good singer, cos everybody joined in. And they were all shoutin 'More hot water! More hot water!' It wis good. It wis baths. I canna mind how much it cost. But I enjoyed that … that was your bath for the week …

In St Mary Street, where my grandparents lived at first, you went up in the attic, right, so you had to come down the wooden stairs, along the plettie, down one flight of stairs to the outside toilet. When you got there, either somebody had stole all the paper – which was newspaper cut into squares – or somebody [had] stole the candle.

The attic was that small you could stand in your bed and piss in the sink. There was one room with an alcove for a bed, and you had a cooker, a wee cupboard, a bunker for the boy comin up wae the coal, a table in the middle and the fire. That wis it. One room. They lived in the one room … Ah never went doon tae the toilet. Can you imagine gaun doon thae cauld stairs? No way! Pish in the sink [laughs]. Well, you had potties in that daes and if you needit a shit ye just did it in the pottie. But ither than that, naw.

Bob has been describing the home of his grandparents off Lochee Road, outwith the Hawkhill. The next extract begins with his memory of the tenements opposite Sinderins.

Bob Fotheringham (b.1945)

Thae tenements were quite toffee-nosed because they all had toilets inside. Then, when ye got past Peddie Street, that's when it wis all factories and tenements like Bernard Street, ken .... We were laughin aboot corn beef legs. Women used tae sit in front o the fire and their legs would be all marbly like corn[ed] beef and that's hoo it got [called] corn beef legs.

Anne Piggott (b.1939)

Cos it wis open fires and ye used tae sit close tae the fires cos that wis the only heatin, an it wis ah marled: pink an broon lookin. Oh, it wis pitiful.

Anne McDonald (b.1946)

There wisnae any comfort. I mean your sink wis [in] your sittin room. Thir wis nae luxury: toilet on the stairs. You had to got to Miller's Wynd for a bath. You went in and got bathed. ... if you were in number six the taps were outside so you had to get someone to add hot water from outside. [laughs] But thir wis nae luxury: far from it ... . They're all spoilt now, aren't they? I think they're all too spoiled, ah the kids an ahthing. Even my kids are spoiled. But as I say, that's what I remember.

There wis nae TV. Naebuddy had TVs. Mah grannie in Bernard Street wis the first one to have a TV. She was an invalid. And I remember this teeny wee thing, an it wis only for aboot an hour a day ... . We just used to sit an watch it, all spots an thingies. We used tae stare an hope something would come on. But it never [did]. [laughs]

Then I remember gettin a wee record player, a Decca. You were able to go an buy records. Meh first record bought wis the Beatles LP. I always remember. Wish I'd kept it. The four faces on the front ... but my brothers had bought other records, like Elvis [Presley].

Peter Taylor (b.1900)

A lot of the people in the tenements were allowed a certain amount of scope by the factors. Some of them had a lean-to at the back and kept pigeons.

Quite a common sight was the washing slung from one tenement to another. Sometimes there was a pole in the [back] green and your washing stretched from the house window to the pole.

Anne McDonald (b.1946)

The back o oor tenement, we had a bit o grass an we didna hae the greenies [poles]. Ye hed tae pull the pulley fae your windae for yer washin. It wis a big pole but fae ahbuddy's kitchen windae there wis a rope went ower tae the big pole an ahbuddy had een at each windae, ken. That's the way ye put yer washin oot.

Along with low wages and poor living conditions came, of course, the constant struggle to make ends meet. The next set of extracts consider some of the ways in which people sought to do this and reminds us again of the vital contribution the berry money made to the family.

Peter Taylor's reminiscences go back to the 1920s, and even before that. He had an insight into the living conditions of some of the poorest Dundonians through the voluntary work he did with the St Vincent de Paul[164] charitable organisation for the less fortunate:

Peter Taylor (b.1900)

We visited people and they were very poor. The national security at that time was the parish council and they called it 'the grubbers'. They got a very little sum of money and the inspectors … came round to assess you for your need. If you had a good piece of furniture, say a piano or the old horn gramophone, they would suggest that you sold these and get some money, so as to protect your negotiation for aid. That was in the 1912–14 period. We had a lot of different characters who were poor, but very clean. Some of the houses you went to were kept very clean … . The poorhouse, at that time there was one in the east end of Dundee and then latterly there was one in the west end. We called them 'grubbers'. At that time people had very little. But they demanded very little.

The means test was aptly named, though scarcely developed, as this next example shockingly illustrates, from Billy Kay's excellent *Odyssey* series:

Sarah Craig
During the winter months, if you didn't have anything and applied what they would term as social security now, but it was the breadline, you might as well say. There was this Mr Allan that was here in the town. He run this looking after the poor, and if he came in and he looked round their house – 'Can ye no sell this, can ye no sell that?' – necessities. But eh, of course, you would say 'I need that'. They would even lift the lid of where you kept your coal – an if you had one bit o coal, you never got any coal.[165]

Jim Devlin (b.1933)
People – after the war – had to squat, what they called squatters, because there was no houses. They hadn't built any of the schemes … all these buildings were condemned. They cut off the water, electric, gas or whatever. They never had electric, it was just gas. And somebody opened one [house] up, went in and lived in it, and it became a big thing in Dundee. People squatted in all the empty tenements. Whole streets that had been closed for demolition. Crescent Lane was one of them.

Peter Taylor (b.1900)

Dundee had plenty of pubs and pawnshops, but the pawnshops were really a godsend to the working people. I mean, wages were very low at the time and you'd big families ... [T]he families' good things, their shirts and costumes an that [went] into the pawn on the Monday. Then, on the Saturday when you got your pay they were bought out and you were dressed for your Saturday and Sunday. But you had to pay interest, of course ... . Some better-off people pawned their jewellery. And some didn't lift it out and it was unredeemed then and sold at a sale.

Anne McDonald (b.1946)

And ye had the pawnshop, ken, on the Hahky. Ye went up a closey an the pawnshop was there. I think mum used tae lift me up and set there. Ain o the suits would go in on a Monday and get picked up again on a Friday or a Saturday ... . Ma dad's suit.

Was that well patronised?

Yes. A lot o fowk said that they never yaised the pawnshop but they did, ken whit Eh mean. Sad, eh, no tae admit that ... . Long ago it wis sleazy like. Nebuddy wid tell they were gaun tae the pawnshop, but my mum didna bother.

Bernadette Dailly (b.1954)

We'd a pawnshop quite near us on the Hawkhill ... . But my mum worked in Dickson's pawnshop that was on the corner of Temple Lane, or the West Port.[166] She worked there for a long time. She actually got her engagement ring there [laughs].

One of the ladies I spoke to said a lot more people went to the pawn than might admit it.

They did. Well, I know my dad, that's how mum met dad ... . He used to go every Friday and get the goods out and then on a

Monday go back and put his Sunday suit in. He would take it back to the pawnshop. I think that was quite common, because they didn't have any money like. I think they used the pawnshop in those days quite a lot. Not when mum and dad were married, but when they were younger, before they got married.

Was there any stigma to that?

I think it was just part of life. The way of life in those days. Most working-class people, that's what they would of had to do.

Before the days of fitted kitchens and white goods, washing clothes was an altogether more complicated affair:

Anne McDonald (b.1946)

Wednesday, I came from school [and would then] go and book a white machine and a coloured machine for Thursday – when my mum used to go to the washing. I'd come home [Thursday] and she'd push the pram wae the two big baskets on it wae rope, and I used tae help her push it up Miller's Wynd, cos that's where the washing wis.

What else would you take?

The Sunlight soap powder and the washing board. Then, in the wee cubicles there was a thing like for boiling your clothes. You put it on. And you could actually buy powder.

Was there a lot of crack in the washy?

Oh, aye. A lot of thievin as well. I remember my mum … . She pulled [this thing] oot, we used tae call it 'the horse', and it wis all hot rails. Mum put all the shirts on it. And my mum didna smoke or anything, but she went awa oot to get something and when she came back she said to me, 'Anne, go an check, say 23' [the number of the rail]. I went over and there was nothing on it. Somebody had stolen all the shirts, ken, all the laddies' shirts.

This next informant recalled her formative years in Peddie Street where her tenement had the drying green round the back and your clothes were hung out from your own back window:

Maureen Gardiner (b.1936)
That wis where you did your washing. There wis a boiler, and a fire that you lit underneath it. An then, I can't remember how it was dried, but there usually was a mangle. You took [the washing] upstairs, and we had a pulley that went out the window, and that's where you hung it. We were on the top floor [laughs] and, I mean, my mum and dad both worked so I used to be hanging out the washing. And this man that lived in Tait's Lane, [he] was a friend of ours, and shouted to me, 'Get back in there or you'll be falling right out!' The windows, they were loose, you know. That was a different type of life, really.
Did everyone know their neighbours?
Everyone knew their neighbours, yeah. People on the ground floor kept the closes clean and the people upstairs scrubbed the stairs. They were scrubbed, not just mopped or wiped.[167]

This next extracts highlight the role of the mother, wider family and social network in ensuring that chores and the domestic routine were kept in good order:

Chic Milne (1923–2017)
Who got the job o settin the fire?
Oh, that wis ma mother's job, really. Women nearly did everything in these days … . But that hoose in Montrose didna have any water in it. Ma mother didna have any water in it. Ma mother had tae go downstairs for water and bring everything up. The toilet wis ootside and the runnin water wis ootside.

Anne McDonald (b.1946)

So when you had an idea of what you mother was doing ... what was her routine?

Well, I always remember she was up at six in the morning and away for rolls. Because she worked, and my brothers worked. So, she was away up for the rolls: 'rain, hail, sleet or snow', as they say. Away up to Wallace's, and doon, butterin the rolls for the laddies to go oot to work. Then me and my brother would get up and we'd hae a roll and a cup o tea, a bit toast – it wis done at the fire wi a fork. I don't like toast two-sided, I like it one-sided. Because I think I wis used to it. Then me and him would leave together and go away to school. We never went in for [school] dinners cos my mum worked six till ten across the road. She had a cleanin job in the morning, at Chalmers – who had the shop at the top of Kincardine Street. She was always in for us at dinnertime. You got soup, or a Wallace's pie – cos it wasn't expensive.

Maureen Gardiner (b.1936)

Grannies would be important, yeah. My grannie was a bit bad on her legs, but then she'd lived in Glasgow and had her family in Glasgow. She was Dundee originally, but married a Glaswegian. He worked in the shipyard and he got TB. So he was in his bed with TB, she had four kids, so all she could do was go out [to find work].

She took in washing, she took in ironing, she scrubbed people's stairs, she did everything she could. Because they didn't get any money, and under no circumstances would they go on the Parish ... . They wouldn't do that. So she did four or five different jobs, just to get a wee bit of money coming in. She came back to Dundee after her husband died and that was when she got the house across the road from us. In those days though, families all seemed to have houses round about each other.

Children too had their own chores and each one pitched in, especially with big families:

Therese Devlin (b.1957)

Well, me myself, I would do as little as possible [laughs] being the youngest girl out of five and the four big sisters. But no, we all had our own chores, eight kids, you all had things to do. Mostly washin the dishes and dryin the dishes, tidyin up. My oldest brother wis stuck in the middle of five girls and his chore wis cleanin the shoes wae his big apron. [He'd] polish the shoes every night, for the whole family.[168] That wis his job, and in the mornins he'd deliver newspapers. So he'd be up early, and then rush off to Lawside Academy.

Mary Angus (b.1940)

When I was at Hawkhill School, which is now lovingly called Blackness, for the whole of my seven years at that school there was only about two people had a blazer in my class … . If you had a summer dress, in the winter you just wore a woollen jersey over the top and, you know, three-quarter length socks and wellies … . I had an auntie who was only six years older than me, she was at secondary school. And I was quite big for my age and I used to get Auntie Agnes's clothes. I never had a school skirt as such, it was only whatever ma mum could put us in to school …[169]

Ma brothers were forever having to get patches in their trousers because they were throwing themselves about the playground saving goals and that. One time, one o ma brothers came in and the sole of his shoe was hanging off, and she was gonna kill him. We always had a [cobbler's shoe] last, ye know, for three different sizes of feet … . And ma father used to buy leather and he used to draw round the shoe … sole and heel our shoes and everything … . Put on the heels to save women's shoes. We used to have them, and that wis your life.

If we were poor we weren't aware of it, ye know. I didn't know there wis fee-paying schools or anything when I wis young. I only realised … that there wis a town [when] I wis in somebody's house (we used to go messages for a lot of the older people round about) … and that was the first time I encountered *The Courier & Advertiser*. And I saw Princess Elizabeth and Princess Margaret, well it wis the Queen at that time, comin out of Draffens[170] … I remember I said … 'What is Draffens …?' Because I didn't know. You didn't have to know there was a town.

Tradition, change and transition is also imprinted on the memories of those who recalled the domestic arrangements for cooking and the food people ate:

Maureen Gardiner (b.1936)

We had coal fires and I can actually remember when we first got a gas cooker in [laughs]. My grandma, who lived across the road, they still had the big range, [with a] grate that you had to blacklead and the coal fire in the front. At the side of it was an oven. That was where she did her baking. And it was from the heat of the fire that baked things.

Then there was a hook that she hung her soup pan on and she just used to put all the bits 'n pieces that were left over, bones an things, into that to make stock.

Bob Fotheringham (b.1945)

Aye, ma grannie had a cast-iron kale pot. She always made kale[171] on a Monday, steeped all the peas an everything on a Sunday night and a joint an ah this kind o thing, so the second day's soup wis even better. Ye could stand yer spuin in it; it widna fa doon it wis that thick. Kale broth. [This] soup was more barley mix, no like tomato soup. That's like water. This was thick, like Scotch broth, similar.

And then, when ye went to Broughty Ferry, ye used tae bring ah the mussels hame an cook them in the pot. Ye can steam them ... and the shell opens. That's afore ah the mussel beds disappeared. There wis loads o mussel beds on the beach ... and I used tae gan doon the Stannergate for them ...

So the broth you described, wis that a staple o your diet?

Yeah, definitely, like, you had the same every day.[172] You'd soup and a Wallace's peh [pie]. Monday, at night, we went to the chip shop across the road, Schiavetta's, the chip shop in Lawrence Street. On Tuesday, when you came back from work, I think it wis liver. Anyway, every day wis the same each week. It never really changed.[173]

Anne McDonald (b.1946)

I never ever seen ma ma with a cookery book. You'd just hear somebody sayin 'I made this': 'Well, how did ye make it?', and ahbuddy telt each other. But maistly, when I think aboot it, ye lived out the chipper and Wallace's pie shop.[174] Ken whit Ah mean? My mum wis too busy to cook ...

Aye, she wis aye workin, or she'd make a big pot of soup and a big pot of rice [pudding]. But then, at teatime, a fish supper wis cheap, no what it's like now. Ah mean ahbuddy went. An ye either got a puddin supper, a fish supper, a fish-cake supper. That wis a cheap wey o eatin, but no now it's no.

Bernadette Dailly (b.1954)

There was the chip shop right across from us, Bastianelli's. That was on the Hawkhill, at the corner of the Hawkhill and Mountpleasant. They were there. And I remember a fire. I think one of the chip pans had gone up ...

Dad did all the cookin on a Sunday. Mum never ... . And he would bake. He was great with pastry, made beautiful pastry.

I suppose that's how it went round the family more, because he did it all himself. But dad would do, on a Sunday, maybe chicken, I think, and latterly meat loaf.

You'd know what day of the week it was because Monday would be tatties an mince, Tuesday would be hotpot, Wednesday would be stovies,[175] Friday was always fish. You always got fish on a Friday because, again, a Catholic family, you couldn't eat meat on a Friday. So even your soup at lunchtime would maybe be just margarine … to give it a flavour, and maybe some vegetables …

Another memory is, whenever it wis somebody's birthday ma dad would make a clootie dumpling. And they were the most delicious dumplings you ever had. They'd put silver sixpences and thrupennies in them, and [these] were wrapped in paper inside your dumplin …

And then, every week, ma mum would get two bottles o lemonade. It would be plain lemonade, because you didn't get the flavours at the time, and that wis between eight o us. You can imagine how much we got to drink.

Bernadette's dad also made the Christmas dinner for 15 hungry mouths. Usually it was turkey.[176] He also made Christmas pies with puff pastry and at New Year made his own steak pie. The maternal side of the family visited at Christmas and the paternal side at New Year. There were memories of other customs associated with New Year too:

Bernadette Dailly (b.1954)

I was too young to go out an about but I remember my sister came in, on probably the last Hogmanay we would of been on the Hawkhill, and she had the kippers wae the fancy ribbons on them, you know. Dressed kippers, yeah. That would be like a first foot[177] and she maybe brought in a bit of coal and the pea busters.[178] That would be down in the Overgate, and they'd bring them up to the Hawkhill.

Maureen Gardiner (b.1936)

You trailed all over Dundee. And at the bottom of the Hilltown there used to be like, stalls, all down there and they had red herring dressed up and dressed white puddings, and there were all the things that you were going to first foot with.[179] They had quite a lot of bits an pieces for you to take round the houses to first foot.

Somebody always used to bring me a red herring or a kipper and you used to hang it on the back of the door and it stayed there until the next year [laughs] when you took it down and put the other one up... It was dressed in crepe paper with, like, skirts and hats. ... The head was still on. They were all dried up.

But first of all, before we started on the walks, we went down to the city square and there were crowds down there, all waiting for the bells. When the bells went everybody wished everybody else a Happy New Year and cheered. ... Then they all started out on their walks. No cars in these days. You walked everywhere, all over the town, until about seven o'clock the next morning.

In the next extracts we hear more about the pea busters, a Dundee speciality that was a year-round treat:

Mary Angus (b.1940)

Then, as we got older, every fifth week we got taken down the Hawkhill to the Overgate. where they sold busters. You went into this tent and the woman had a brazier and a great big pot of chips and peas, a pile of old saucers and a pile of old side-plates, all chipped and scratched, and you got a buster. When the chips were ready she used to shout 'Step insides now! Step inside'.

In the summer, of course, you were roasting – because you were under this canvas and the fire was going. She used to put her hand half over the plate and throw the chips on. How she didn't get burned, we'll never know. Then a ladle of peas, but by the time she took her hand away it had all flattened out and you weren't getting as much as you thought you were. Thruppence or fourpence. And she had a white enamel pail that wes all bashed, cold water, and the plates just got dipped in and dried with her jute overall [laughs]. … As ma mother used to say: 'Nobody died a winter yet'.

Anne McDonald (b.1946)

My sister-in-law's grannie, that was her buster stall down there and my sister-in-law used to work there on a Saturday … . It was funny, see when you look back now you wouldnae eat it on the plates because the saucers were all cracked an the plates were cracked. You never noticed that. But nowadays nobody would eat that if it was on a plate like that.

The stall was like a tent, a canvas tent wae this brazier in the middle and it was like wooden seats all round … . Then you would just sit down with your saucer and get a fork or spoon … . See in the winter, it was warm. The brazier was on in the summer and you used to sit there roastin. But in the winter it was cosy.

Christmas customs were far less lavish than in more recent times:

Maureen Gardiner (b.1936)

My dad was in the Blackness Foundry, on the munitions. My mum worked in the laundry in Tait's Lane, which is the next street along from Peddie Street. My dad thought this was a good wage. He got three pounds ten shillings a week. … I know that he was on some committee for leisure because we had excursions. Because he was on the committee he met in with people and was able to get some little toys and things for Christmas, cos there was nothing really. Ma dad made things. He made little carts with wooden blocks, all beautifully rounded and shaped and painted, and a hen shape pulling them ... [I remember one year] I got the surprise of my life because usually you got a *Dandy* book, a *Beano* book, an apple and an orange and a penny in the toe of your stocking. You didn't get very much else. So this year I got a tea set, because he'd managed to get this from being on this committee.

This next snapshot of the Hawkhill reveals the interface between town and gown at a charities' procession before Dundee became a university in its own right:[180]

Therese Devlin (b.1957)
I remember it being all the old cobbles on the road and one of my memories is of the old lorries going up and down. And I do remember the student processions they used to have. I thought it was from St Andrews University, because they used to wear the red capes. [There were] all the different floats. We would get to hang out the window and throw pennies, which would be [a] very rare [treat] from my mum, trying to get them to land on the floats.

Capes were the famous red, or scarlet, gowns worn by students. The late J. J. Robertson was a law academic and canon law expert at the University of Dundee. He had graduated from St Andrews with an MA in 1953 and the LLB[181] in 1956. At that time law students were apprenticed to a legal firm while still studying at Queen's College in Dundee:

Jim Robertson (b.1932)
And did the college in Dundee have similar colours to the St Andrews gown?
Exactly the same, except, I think, instead of a maroon collar they had a blue collar. But the gowns were still worn in Dundee when I went there. I didn't wear one and very few students actually wore them, because it was in a city – they weren't worn.

Hawkhill resident, Anne McDonald, and her family moved from Bernard Street to their flat above the famous Tavern pub which was, in its later years, a magnate for folk musicians and artists:

Anne McDonald (b.1946)
It was okay, a bit noisy at times, but okay. We used tae look out the window and watch everybody coming out drunk. And my dad was one of them [laughs]. We were second floor with the attics above us, because we were right above the Tavern.

Duncan Soutar (b.1946)
I think it was the Tav that had a folk session on a Saturday afternoon. And the bar would be mobbed wae people watchin the fitba on the telly and the wee snug had a session going on.[182] There wid be about twenty-five or thirty people crammed into this snug, tryin tae play music and it wis brilliant. It wis a wee bit crowded, ye know, the bow o the fiddle wis going in fowk's ears an ahthing. Ah remember they didnae hae a ladies' toilet, so if ye took yer girlfriend wae ye, ye stood guard at the door while she went in!

Bernadette Dailly (b.1954)
Ma dad worked in the Ratay pub Friday, Saturday, Sunday so mum and dad weren't one for going out. They didn't drink. Ah

think ma mum wis about 45 before she had her first drink … .
We usetae have a looky in the Ratay sometimes and you'd just
see [the men], only men were allowed in it, and you'd see
sawdust on the floor.

Vintage Dundee pubs were on the radar of this next informant
whom I regret recording only once in January, 1983:

Peter Taylor (b.1900)

The Black Doors in [North] Tay Street.[183] It's away now of
course. Everything was painted black. The doors were all painted
black and half o the window was painted black so you couldn't
look in. It used to get a lot of rough people, especially tinkers.
They used to take flagons in and get porter. They went up the
pend at number 10 Tay Street, sat round the back and drank it.
That's 1914–15, for I was called up wae conscription three years
later … . When you left Tay Street and went down the left hand
side you got the Woodbine Bar; after you passed that, at the top
of Long Wynd, it was Yeoman's pub. After that you'd the en-
trance to our school, St Andrew's Primary. You passed there,
then you came to the Harp & Thistle. That was a big pub. At
the end of [North] Lindsay Street you had the Mercat Cross,
another pub, and across from that, J. B. Lawson's. Down from
that was Menzies, but no other pubs. On the other side was
plenty: The Pump, The Swan, The Steeple.

One of Dundee's oldest pubs was Coyle's in the Hawkhill.
That was a great rum shop. When people had a cold they all
went to Coyle's for a glass; or a gill, of rum. MC rum; it was
well known.[184]

Duncan Soutar (b.1946)

Who usually patronised the snugs?
Well, the snug was basically the carry-out section in a pub. Ye

didn't go into the main pub if ye wanted a bottle o beer or yer jug filled up. It was also where, if they'd a couple o seats, where ladies might go in, because in general women weren't either welcome in the bar, or it was sniffed on for women to go into pubs. My grannie wis never in a pub in her life.

What was the boley?

The little window that ye stuck yer heid through and shouted for drink. It was a window, a space, often with a little counter – usually on the end of the bar rather than in the bar itself. So the barman could turn round and see you at the boley and bring your order … take the jug off yer bairn to fill it up, so that the bairn could take it back to the hoose. That's going back to the days before I was born.

Anne McDonald (b.1946)

I never remember my mum haen nights oot cos on Saturday nights in Bernard Street, at the bottom, a man used to come with an accordion an ah the women would just sit there and we would ah play. They'd maybe hae a wee drink and maybe a wee dance at the bottom o the street … . Men went tae pubs. Very rarely did ye get women gaun. It wis ah men.

In Peter Taylor's time it was not just the women that danced:

Peter Taylor (b.1900)

When I wis a bit younger, in Session Street, up the West Port there – I was born there in 1900. Now there was a shed there and this old gentleman, Mr Herd, he took in wood and cut it up into bunches. Now, [at] one time Russians came with big brown bears and they used to be put up in his shed. I've seen a couple of big brown bears in that shed.

They came out and, in the street, would dance round a big pole. The bear was on a long chain, of course, and it had a wee cup round it where you put pennies and ha-pennies. That's away around 1912 …

There was another character in Barrack Street, Jess Jenkins, and she lived there. She was a wee bit doubtful in character, but a good person. She volunteered to go in the old Palace in the Nethergate – it was a variety theatre – and she went in and boxed a bear.

Robert Douglas, in his book *Night Song of the Last Tram*, evokes the twilight activity of Glasgow's street gambling which was very much part of life in industrial Scotland. Similar activities were also to be found in Dundee:

Chic Milne (1923–2017)

There were bookies' runners who used to stand at the end of tenement closes and take bets, even if it was illegal. The police knew about the activity and would crack down on it every now and again. They didn't stamp it out. They'd warn the runners the day before that they'd be picked up, so there was a short-lived lull. Those lads acted like spies or secret agents and used to have a leather bag to collect bets. They gave the punters a nom de plume: mine was Chic 24. They'd write [the bets] down on anything, [for instance] the back of an old Woodbine packet. Latterly some gave you a proper ticket with a number on it.

[That] all fizzled out when the bookies didn't need runners.[185] They became legal and you could hand over a bet, any bet – a penny, tuppenny, thruppence. … My father used to bet by post in Montrose. In Dundee, the bookies' runners were practically found on every street because they worked a certain area and had to turn out daily at the same spot.

In his memoir, that in part evokes his upbringing in the Gorbals, Andy Coogan asserts that local bookmakers paid off the local bobbies – who knew perfectly well what was going on with illegal street betting: the reason being that the police enjoyed a punt too.[186]

An aspect of urban life that was very different from the countryside were the street sounds which accompanied daily life. These would change over time and in the following extracts we hear about this, including the sounds associated with the jute mills:

Anne McDonald (b.1946)

You used to hear the horse and cart bringing coal. No often cars, because there wasnae a lot. Nobody had cars really. Trams came up the Blahky, no the Hawkhill. If the door wis open you'd hear the racket from the mills, the noise o machinery. I used to say to mum it's a wonder you're no deaf wae that, because a lot o people sign-languaged. You couldnae hear. It wis too noisy.

If the big door wis open, like o Cairdy's there, you'd look in and see all the machines clatterin and I usetae go, 'I'll never work in there', and I never did.[187] Mum said 'You'll never go and work in a mill'. And I never did.

At Cairdy's you heard the bummer going. That wis when it wis time for everybody to go out for their dinner and the same at night when the factory closed … . Abdee would come oot dinnertime. The pavements would be packed with people. And blokes sittin ootside if it wis sunny, ken, with their pieces, stuff like that'.

Duncan Soutar (b.1946)

The bummer wis anytime, Ah think, work changed. So, if work was to start there wis a bummer and if work wis to stop there wis a bummer. So if you heard a bummer on your way to work you had to be quick, or there was a chance you could be docked your wages for being late. There was also a chance, in some of the mills, if you were more than a few minutes late you didn't get in [at all], so you lost a day's work.

You had to be in the complex. A mill wisna just a building, it wis a series o buildings. Some o the bigger mills had many buildings, with roads inside. The main gate had a gate-keeper on it and once the bummer had gone for the start of the day he would shut that gate … You can still see, to this day, a lot of the existing tenements are in walking distance of whaur the mills would of been.

Peter Taylor (b.1900)
The west end was mostly jute mills. They were set up before the turn o the [twentieth] century … . That's why most of the population were concentrated in a small area – to be near the mills. Dundee was very congested as regards housing.

Mary Angus (b.1940)
Well, ma grannie stayed in a tenement where the Ryehill Health Centre is today. It's called Ryehill Lane and … och, that wis like a warren of people. If we were going along at ma grannie's, to see if she needed any messages, and you said, 'Could I go to the toilet?' – well, you'd get the key. And she would say, 'Keep that watery clean, Eh'm no haen the neebors speakin aboot me', You were frightened to go!

It used to be quite foggy with all the jute mills, the chimneys going, and it wis quite bad. If it was foggy – you got the smog.[188]
What quality of light would you have had?
We had gas light on the mantelshelf and it had a gauze bulb that you lit and you could adjust it.[189] If it broke on a Saturday night, or a Sunday, the policeman's box was at the end of the street at Sinderins. You went along and just waited for a policeman and they took your name, and then on the Monday you bought one and you replaced it and put it back.

Anne McDonald (b.1946)

… the gas, and the coal fires, and the mills. Ye wonder how we survived tae this day. We were just used tae it. Mind you, we had some good summer days. And ye had the tar on the roads. And ye used tae burst the bubbles and used to get margarine to get the tar off yer hands.

Ye wouldnae be bare feet though?

Eh! Bare feet! Never had a shoe. They called me the Barefoot Contessa efter the film wae [Ava] Gardner in it. Never had a shoe on. Ah'd sannies and when there wis a hole in the sole ye cut out cardboard and put it in and [that] made it last a little longer. What a sad life, Roger. [laughs] Sad.

When they were younger, work experience in the city was not as readily available for girls as it was for boys.[190] Perhaps they would run messages for older folk, then, as teenagers, they might pick up waitressing or domestic jobs. And, of course, in the summer there was the berries. In this next extract Therese Devlin reminds us of the benefit of the berries income, for the whole family:

Therese Devlin (b.1957)

Just in the summertime, we went to the berries. As I say, there was eight of us and that's how, when we moved to our new house we were able to get a fridge, got the phone installed – just wae us all going to the berries, and to buy all our school clothes after the summer.

We went to Joseph Leonard out in Longforgan … a lot of memories. I'd hate it. We used to get sent out with your packed lunch. You'd open it up and get the surprise of your life! In your sandwich – we called it a 'piece' – we got raspberry jam. You were pickin raspberries! – and it kind of put ye off raspberry jam for life … [laughs]

We'd go with our good clothes on in the bus and get

changed when we got there, and she would give you any old stuff to change into if ye didn't have anything. Ah always remember coat hooks and all these old coats hanging up. If it was heavy rain, or rain of any sort, you'd put the jackets on, put your arm through the jacket and in between you'd come against all these cobwebs and everything.

Then you'd have to tie them with a string, … to stop the water trying to drip down your arms. It was horrible. Ah don't know what we looked like? A load o ragamuffins, I suppose. Just goin out picking wae the luggie and the string round yer waist. That's one o my horriblest memories. The more berries you put in yer luggie the heavier it got and it just dug into yer waist. And ye'd tae trail back doon the dreel [wae] yer bucket, empty it and bring the bucket back up. You can gather I loved the berries [laughs].

That's what I did anyway. As I say, my brother did deliverin the papers, and I'm sure he did milk as well at some stage.

Willie Robertson has written about his memories of delivering milk in 60s Dundee and has a hilarious take on the subject which is well worth reading.[191] From an earlier era this next contributor goes back to the horse and cart days, in the coastal town of Montrose.

Chic Milne (1923–2017)

That wis ma first job. Ah think Ah got a shillin a week for it. … I usetae gaun oot in the mornin early, aboot mibbe five, meet the milkman, Andra Clark. Ye would meet him at a certain place in the town and he wid hev yer milk made up intae tin cans. I think I'd only two customers the first time I went on this job … . Whoever wis gettin the milk usetae leave oot a jug at the doorstep, wae mibbe a saucer or a cover over the top of it.

I had this tin can o milk and poured the milk into the jug, or what was ever left at the door. That wis the way it wis delivered. I always mind when I got my start on the first mornin he says, 'There's a bit o white soap, tae ye'. I said, 'Whit's this white soap for Mr Clark?' and he says, 'Well, sometimes the cans leak'. And ye just put the soap into the can where it leaked, an that sealed the hole, until it got too big and the soap wouldnae stop it like … but it didnae taste the milk.

Andrew Fenwick recalled his time as a paper delivery boy:

Andy Fenwick (b.1964)
Did you have a job as a boy apart from the berries?
Ah did, yeah. A newspaper round. And Ah used to do that in between school and after school. Ah used to do a paper round on Lochee Road. It was quite a hard paper round actually, like a double round, Lochee Road first and then Rankine Street, which was up a steep brae with a lot of tenements, very high tenements on Lochee Road …
What was the most popular paper?
The most popular paper Ah reckon wis the *Evening Telegraph* and probably the *Courier, Dundee Courier.*
What about on a Sunday?
The Sunday Post … by far.

Another job was with the football pools and in this next extract we learn about this and also about the mining which replaced fishing as the main industry in Buckhaven:

Brian Melville (b.1956)
The football pools. That wis a big thing in these days. Men used to bet on the football pools and, Ah mean, it was something that was seen as being acceptable. Ye know, if ye went tae

the bookies and spent aw yer money on horses and things [that might be frowned on] … whereas football coupons wis seen tae be something more respectable. Ye were bettin on the outcome o fitba rather than horses or dugs or anything; it's a by-product of a sport rather than the sport being there for bettin.

Ah mean, Ah wis aboot 13 when Ah usetae dae that, an Ah usetae go oot on a Thursday night and a Friday night. But Ah suppose it wis quite good experience for me because Ah got tae handle money. And Ah had tae cash up at night, and have all the right money. Ye learned aboot change … . Ye had tae be fairly honest and fairly sharp when ye were givin out change and things for people … . That wis the only part-time job Ah hed. Ah can remember it bein dark and daen it in the winter months, because football wis a winter game. Ah can remember always doin it at night, when it was always dark and wet and cauld an rainin.

Ah mean, Ah usetae do it roond aboot ma home town, so Ah knew a lot o people whose houses Ah wis gaun tae … Buckhaven anyway, what had happened [there] wis ye hed a fishin community which wis seventy per cent o the trade in the town and it fairly quickly, over a number of years once they found more coal in Denbeath, the whole town's function changed completely. And it became a pit town because most of the men [then] worked in the pit.

From ma point of view, ma grandad was underground and he spent fifty years, more than fifty years, underground. So it's like, Ah can remember him havin coal-dust in his hands and havin blue marks on his face where he'd got an injury and the coal-dust had got in and sealed over. And he has these blue scars on his hands and his face.

That's kind of how an industry like mining lasts and gets into the blood of a community as well. Because Buckhaven had very much gone from having one identity, that of a fishing community, to having another identity which was a mining community. So there was quite a change of people's outlook.

Message boys pushing heavy ton-weight bikes loaded with goods were once a common enough sight and provided employment for the fittest youngsters:

Bob Fotheringham (b.1945)

Oh, that was Lawrence Street and Polepark, because I worked for the butcher's – as a message boy – on Wednesdays and worked Saturdays. Then I worked for Laird's[192] delivering messages for them. They were on the corner o Polepark and Fyffe Street.

Did you push a bike?

Yes. I hated Wednesday mornings because I got up, washed, got out and had to go to Downfield, right. Now that's a long way and I had to push the bike up Rankine Street, then go all the way through Beechwood, down the Kingsway … but see comin back doon Rankine Street. The feet on the bar, free-wheel right down because there wasn't much traffic coming down Lochee Road and you could go right down and right down Polepark. Brilliant!

Fixed gear?

Naw, naw, wis it buggery! Naw, naw, just an ordinary bike. It didn't have any gears on it. It wis brilliant comin back doon the brae. Whoosh!

Likewise, this next memory from an informant whose father had been in the grocery business:

John H. Beaton MBE (b.1937)

He'd been at Johnston's Stores [grocer and wine merchant] in the Wellgate when I was a laddie of message bike age. I used to

get the messages and load up and have to go on a Saturday
morning ride up the Hilltown, and with no gears on the
message bike and a fair load.

You just didn't know any different. You did it because the
alternative was to go around Victoria Road and come up Main
Street. And so I used to do that and that was me. I was away
racing the next morning, getting up at six o'clock in the
morning for a time trail out the Perth Road.

The Hilltown is one of the steepest streets in the city of
Dundee. It was a very tough ascent but one which was a spring-
board for John's later success as a racing cyclist. He was a Scottish
Junior and Senior level champion, as well as Captain of the British
Army on the Rhine cycle team. His early work experience remains
a tangible link however:

John H. Beaton MBE (b.1937)

When ma father had his own [grocer's] business, especially in
the Hawkhill, he had customers. And the furthest away
customer was the matron of Huntly Castle, the borstal, a bad
boys' school. And she had a little business going that she would
get jam and sell jam to the laddies, because they just got their
basic portions and all the rest of it. Guys could always get
biscuits and crackers but they needed something to put on it
and they weren't allowed, so she'd a little business going selling
the jam and marmalade etcetera. I had the job of loading up a
message bike with a big basket, a deep basket. It was such an
unbelievable weight I'd to pump the tyres up solid because of the
weight. I'd no idea. Under ergonomic rulings now, there's not a
hope in hell that you could consider letting a 14-year-old laddie
[ride] with all this weight. If you braked on the bike too hard the
weight of the front threw you over the handlebars. So I used to
have to cycle laden out the Perth Road and then ... Invergowrie,

Longforgan, and then free-wheel, holding onto the brakes gently in case the weight of the basket [would] throw me over. The worst bit was the last bit, the old Huntly Castle. That's where she was based. I had to get up there and I just couldn't cycle, because many of these old castle-type houses had a very steep ramp. There was not a hope in hell that with all the weight in this basket could the bike go up. And I recall that I used to time it when the people were coming, the wardens as you may call them. They would bring a squad o lads in and I can remember the first time there was this chap and he got shouted, 'Get across here and gie the message laddie a hand!' This young lad, he was balded before bald heads or shaven heads were a fashion, and he was solid built. And he just took hold o this basket wae all these jars o jam and I couldn't take some out to lighten it because this was the country house of thieves and it would just disappear. Castle Huntly, ye know. [laughs] He lifted this basket out full. I'd to hold onto the bike. He pulled it out, popped it down and I'll never forget what he said, 'Honest life no agreein wae you?' … And the next job was to get them up the stairs. He'd to help drag them up intae the hallway. The matron came and locked the door so we could take them up some at a time, up to her room and put them on the shelves.

He said to me when I couldn't lift the thing – the huge basket with all the jam … . They weren't supposed to talk in borstal during certain hours, so lifting the thing, he just said, 'Honest life no agreein wae you?' [laughs] You don't forget these things. All these things imprint wae me.

And what value do you think can be attached to nostalgia?
Well, you've got to have learned from the good and the bad that you've done, and nostalgia is recall mainly of the good things. When you think of nostalgia you don't think of the bad things and it does make you thankful that you've been here to partici-pate in these things.

The Hawkhill obviously had a special place in the hearts of the people who grew up there:

Andy Anderson (b.1957)

Well ken what, the Hahky wis like Lochee, it wis like a toon on its own; like a Hilltoon, like Lochee. That's whit it wis like. You lived in a place, everybody knew ye ... you kent everybuddy and everybuddy knew you. It was good. They'd look efter you. Gie ye a packet o crisps, or a bit sweetie now an again, or money. If ye had a penny ye got a big bag o broken biscuits, ken, always something.

Anne McDonald (b.1946)

Naebdee ever hed their doors locked as everybody trusted each other tae be honest, ye know that ...

Ah remember the first time there wis a car in Bernard Street and everybody wis lookin roond and in it. Ma pal, Jenny Little, it wis her dad's car and he usetae tak us a run along the Perth Road and up Blackness Avenue and back doon again. That's the first time ever Ah wis in a car. Eh'd be eight or nine year auld ... . The Hawkhill was ah like lorries, coal lorries an ahthing. Nebdee had cars. If ye had a car it wis a Perth Road toff ... . Eh've always lived at the west end, where Eh wis born. Born in Bernard Street ... . We could o moved to a scheme but mum didna, the laddies didna [want that]. But all my pals from Bernard Street all moved. To Charleston, St Mary's, an some of them went to Beechwood, but we never. We stayed in the west here.

In this final extract, from Alex Lackie, we glimpse how life changed for those who chose to move to more modern housing:

Alex Lackie (b.1957)

So we moved to Mid[193] in 1962, an a fev bedroom hoose. Me an ma wee brother played hide an seek for a year. The hoose wis that fuckin [big]. It wis like livin in a fuckin palace, Eh swear to God.

So, ah o a sudden, eight fowk wae twa bedrooms an an ootside lavvie [went] tae a fev bedroom hoose whaur me an Ricky hed oor ain room, and Peter hed thir ain room, Nancy hed her ain room, mum an dad hed their ain room.

Ricky says 'Coont tae a hunder an came an find us' ... . Took us a fuckin year! [laughs]

NOTES

1   Brexit. An abbreviation of 'British Exit' referring to the UK's decision in 2016 to leave the European Union.

2   Annual lecture in memory of Dr Alan Bruford, an eminent folklorist, Celtic scholar and senior member of staff at the School of Scottish Studies.

3   See Bennett, 2013.

4   Francie Markis and his nephew of the same name, also known as 'the Wonderful Boy', were two worthies who achieved near mythological status in the collective memory of the north-east based on their remarkable feats and exploits brought to fruition by the oral tradition of the Doric. See Rothney, 2011, 17–18.

5   This work was 'Highly Commended' when it was considered by the Michaelis-Jena Ratcliff prize judges.

6   See Leitch, 1993.

7   Sometimes marked on old maps as Fishtown of Usan, a semi-deserted village and former coastguard station, 2½ miles south of Montrose, Angus. Dave Pullar senior was a joiner before taking up wild salmon fishing with his son (also called Dave). His mother's family were fisherfolk from Elie in Fife. His grandfather stayed on the Naughton estate in north-east Fife and Dave fished around Balmerino and the banks of the Tay. See the profile of the Pullars, 'Wild at Heart', by Helen Brown, *The Courier*, 12 April 2011.

8   Contacts would put forward or suggest other people for me to speak to and I would follow-up these recommendations with letters and phone calls.

9   Derick S. Thomson (1921–2012) was a noted poet and Gaelic scholar.

10   See the beautifully evocative memoir of Calum and his collecting career in Seán Ó Súilleabháin's contribution to Maclean, 1975, vii–xvi. Family poems are also included, in particular those by brother Sorley and his 'Elegy for Calum I. Maclean'.

11   The Ferrograph was an early open-reel tape recorder.

12   Donald Archie MacDonald (1929–99) was a gifted and passionate Gaelic folklorist, originally from North Uist. An outstanding bilingual scholar, Donald Archie became acting Director of the School of Scottish Studies before his untimely death in early retirement. Of several obituaries, perhaps the most rounded eulogy was that of Fred MacAulay at Donald Archie's funeral service in Portree. From this we learned that on Donald's maternal line his grandmother was descended from the MacRury clan who were smiths and sword-makers to the Clan Donald.

A few choice words sum up Donald Archie's reach: distinguished, noble, generous, modest and with a sparkle of anger. These in turn made him the complete man. A celebration of his work was selected for *Tocher*, v57 (2003). This was highly appropriate as Donald Archie and Dr Alan Bruford had edited *Tocher* for many years. Donald Archie went the extra mile to make himself available to assist students such as myself, even into retirement.

13   A selection of Peter Morrison's repertoire and potted life story was collected, compiled and edited by Donald Archie MacDonald, MacDonald, 1977. Peter also had stories and songs published over the years in *Tocher*. He was born in Grimsay, one of the North Uist islands and learnt his tales from older tradition-bearers in ceilidh houses. That of Big Calum Matheson from Point was to the fore. His father was born on an island between Grimsay and North Uist. No one lives there today and the old ruin could still be seen in the 1970s. His great-grandmother was fair-haired Mairi from Rona, another island.

Peter left school at the age of 14. For a time he was a railway surfaceman at Gourock, a Merchant Navy-man who made numerous transatlantic voyages, a Lovat Scout who survived the carnage of Gallipoli as well as a stint as an engineer's rigger at the St Stephen's shipyard on the Clyde. As an islandman, he and his family were true pioneers when, for a time after the Second World War, they were sole inhabitants of Heisker (Monach Isles) and the island of Heillsgeir. In May, 1988, Donald Archie MacDonald and I interviewed Peter's son, Lachlan, then aged 64. Lachlan told me in English about the Heisker adventure:

'Father had the idea of four families from Grimsay going out there and starting it all up again. But when it came to the crunch they wouldn't go, so he went on his own and took his family with him. It was a great pity: the scheme was a good one, and had the other three families come in and made it a sort of club effort…. Some would have worked the land and some the sea; … But it was much too difficult for us at that time; it would be a different story, going out today because of the (better) boats and communications'.

See also the interview with Lachlan Morrison in Neat, 2000, 34–61. Interviewing Lachlan at his home, Sandbank, Grimsay, was unforgettable. Donald Archie MacDonald had once been marooned there on a fieldtrip and spent the night in the very hospitable company that was Lachlan Morrison, a quietly spoken, gentle man and philosopher of life.

14   Obituary: Alan Lomax (1915–2002), *The Herald*, 7 August 2002, 18.

15   Jimmy Henderson is one of 22 veteran Scottish journalists who are profiled by oral historian Ian MacDougall in MacDougall, 2013, 386–414. He goes under his full name of James Gunn Henderson.

16   George MacKenzie was a principal lighthouse keeper who had 41 years and 7 months service with the Northern Lighthouse Board, some of that time on pillar rock stations in the Atlantic. I recorded George in late May 1983 at Durness, Sutherland.

17   The winter gelly (tent) was made from hooped boughs or saplins and tarpaulin, if possible.

18   See the Introduction, Leitch, 1988, xi–xxxiii. A later, equally memorable visit was made with artist and musician, M. Anderson.

19   In conversation with Donald Archie MacDonald, 23 June 1995.

20   Grassy stretches of land adjoining the Atlantic seaboard affording excellent grazing, similar to links but usually more level. See Watson, 2012.

21   SA1983.098-100 (each tape was approximately 48 minutes long, 24 minutes each side).

22   The title given to the oldest surviving member of the Church of Scotland.

23   Fraserburgh.

24   Some of Duncan's stories have been published for example, by Craig, in 'Sgielachdan Dhunnchaidh'. (See *Gairm*, vol. 3). See the contribution on Storytelling by Donald A MacDonald in Thomson, 1987, 280–82.

25   Noted from a weekend spent interviewing Donald MacDonald (b.1912) on the island of Eriskay, 15 and 16 September, 1984:

      'My grandfather came from Corrodale on the east side of North Uist. I think it was my grandfather's third eviction. The people were driven out after they'd cultivated the land. I knew of one family who settled here and it was their seventh eviction. You see, Eriskay was regarded as unproductive: stones and rocks. So the people from Barra and Uist were allowed to settle. The nature of the island (topography) meant they'd to turn to the sea although initially they weren't fishermen. They went to the east coast to get jobs on boats and came back … in 1937 there were sixteen herring fishing boats in Eriskay. Barra people and Eriskay [folk] are closer due to the fact that the Barra folk were fishermen, herring fishermen.'

26   Delargy, 1945.

27   James Delargy was Director of the Irish Folklore Commission (IFC). His vision and devotion to this government-funded folklore institution was a major factor in its success. In April 1971 it was reassigned to a Department of Irish Folklore within University College Dublin. Delargy's legacy was world class in terms of traditional oral culture in Ireland. The IFC was started, in 1935, ahead of Scotland's School of Scottish Studies (est. 1951).

28   Murphy, 1973.

29   MacDonald, in Dorson, 1972, 407–30.

30   MacDougall, 1993; MacDougall, 2009.

31   Martin, 2002.

32   *McGregor's Gathering*, BBC Radio Scotland.

33   Kay, 1996.

34   Ives, 1974.

35   Devine, 1979, 344–59 and Devine, 2019.

36   Holmes, Heather, 'Seasonal and Casual Agricultural Workers', in Fenton and Veitch, 2011, 477–502.

37   For information relating to the seasonal migration associated with the grain harvest from the seventeenth century in connection with the Lowden Hairst (Lothian Harvest) see also Sprott, Gavin, Introduction to Fenton and Veitch, 2011.

38 Smout and Wood, 1990, 22.

39 Watson, A., 2011.

40 Watson, N., 2006, 96–97.

41 Cheape and Sprott, 1980, 18.

42 One of the rare descriptions of the flax harvest in process is found in Salmond, 1944. James Bell Salmond [Wayfever] (1891–1958) was a novelist and one time editor of *The Scots Magazine*. *Flower of the Flax* was his first novel. He nurtured prominent Scottish authors James Leslie Mitchell (Lewis Grassic Gibbon) and Neil M. Gunn in their formative years, and also wrote histories of the 51st Highland Division (1953) and the R&A (1956). His range also extended to an excellent book on the Wade roads, poetry and short story writing. A graduate of the University of St Andrews he had served as an officer with the Black Watch during the First World War, before turning to journalism as a career.

43 According to Joe Tindal, this harvest went to Proctor's in Blairgowrie.

44 D. Proctor & Sons Ltd, Ashgrove Works, New Rattray were one of three flax, tow and jute spinners listed in the *Dundee, Forfar and Perth Trades' Directory* for 1934–35.

45 Symon, 1959, 232–33.

46 Robertson, 1973, 106. Skipper Ian Murray (b. 1941, St Andrews) caddied at Balcomie Links, mostly for American clients.

47 Six volumes of Groome's *Ordnance Gazetteer*, vol. 1, c. 1891, 29.

48 Mrs J. Bett, Abernethy, is the entry listed in the *Dundee, Forfar and Perth Trades' Directory* for 1934–35 under the heading of Carting Contractor.

49 Outward migration has been a fact of life for Hebrideans. In the 1880s many able-bodied young Lewis men obtained work on east-coast fishing boats. Likewise, women followed the herring and learned gutting, pickling and kippering from the English girls brought to Stornoway. Such summer work fitted into the rhythm and cyclical nature of crofting between seed-time and harvest.

50 The word 'hailing' in this context does not appear to be glossed in the *SND*. It appears on an early plan of the River Tay dealing with a fishing dispute, from Frankenstein to Balhepburn. RHP3585. Plan by Alex Mitchell, Perth (1840).

51 Hodd, 1974, 282.

52 *New Statistical Account* X (1837), 392. Errol, Perth.

53 The first outbreak of myxomatosis was reported in the UK in 1953. Initially encouraged as a means of culling rabbits, the practice of actively placing sick rabbits in burrows was made illegal in 1954. The disease is believed to have wiped out 99 per cent of rabbits in the UK, although numbers soon recovered.

54 The rabbit pelts were also a valuable resource being used as linings for hats and gloves.

55 A term for stake nets in general.

56 PP Cd. 148.

57 *Clark's Trades Directory, Dundee, c.*1885, 130.

58 For a long time, anglers on Scottish salmon rivers regarded commercial netsmen as their enemy and held them entirely responsible for low catch rates by rod and reel.

59 Heads of the net.

60 Just below five miles NW of Laurencekirk on the fringes of the Howe of the Mearns.

61 Lugworm was used in addition to the more common, mussel bait. See Fenton, A, 'Shellfish as Bait' in Smout, 1992, 137–53. Hay and Bruce, 1985. Angus Martin's poem 'Bait Gathering' from his book *The Larch Plantation* (p.7), captures the nature of the task using a poet's brevity and memorable imagery.

62 Gourdon to the north had a long tradition of sma line fishing.

63 By way of illustration of the strength required for this move I have an image showing one of the large Northumberland cobles being hauled ashore by twelve men at least, six on either side of the ropes which are attached to the large oak wheels of the janker.

64 *Perthshire Advertiser*, 27 June, 1878.

65 Letter to the author from Affleck Gray, Pitlochry, Perthshire, dated 18 August 1995. Affleck Gray was the author of a fascinating book called *The Big Grey Man of Ben Macdhui*, regarding a supposed spectre that haunted the hill.

66 Birnam School Logbook 1874–1930. I am very grateful to Sylvia Robertson for laying at my disposal the fruits of her research into school logbooks of Highland Perthshire.

67 Morrison and Reynolds, 2004, 27.

68 Kinloch Rannoch School Logbook 1937–81.

69 Royal Grammar School Dunkeld Logbook, 1868–1915 (January 1909).

70 Dunkeld School Logbook 1915–30 (June 1916).

71 See Leitch, R. 'Time Out' Leisure in Storrier, 2006, 638–41.

72 (PP Cd. 8731) 1917, report by Mr James Rodger, 1294–95.

73 Fenton, 1994, 4.

74 Michie, 2000, 165.

75 Orr, 1982, 112. Author, broadcaster and respected ecologist, Adam Watson, told me he had worked as a deer ghillie during vacations when he was a student at Aberdeen University. His book *It's a Fine Day for the Hill* captures his youthful exploits and the memorable characters he encountered.

76 Royle, T. 'The Hills are Alive', *Scotland on Sunday* magazine, 15 March 1992, 12–14.

77 Mackenzie, 1995, 116–17.

78 See the comment on sporting estates and their future by Cameron McNeish in his article, 'Scotland End to End', *The Scots Magazine*, November 2012, 23–24. See also Satterley, 2012.

79 In Roman law a deer was *res nullius*: nobody's thing.

80 Kerr, 1986, 111. Arguably all wild land is managed in Scotland and the concept of true wilderness a misnomer.

81 OS one-inch to the mile, Perth and Strath Earn, sheet 63, first published, 1927. GR947327.

82 Wylie, 1932, 51.

83 Douglas and Oglethorpe, 1993, 16.

84 Dickson, 1868–69.

85 OS one-inch, Arbroath and Montrose, sheet 58, first published, 1946. GR692600

'Puggieston Tile Works' (pronounced, Pudgieston). The site of Puggieston (or Pugeston on modern maps) is omitted from the innovative work by Douglas and Oglethorpe in their gazetteer of brick, tile and fireclay works for Angus (p. 52).

86 Smout, 1986, 93–94.

87 Dostoevsky, 2010, 233–34. William McIlvanney's novel, *The Kiln*, is one of the few works to feature a brickworks and those who work there.

88 Cults, two miles out of Ladybank, Fife. *Johnston's Gazetteer of Scotland*, 2nd edition (1958), gives 'limeworks'. See Hume, 1976, 130.

89 Watson, 2010, 19.

90 Patrick MacGill's books such as *Children of the Dead End* (1914), *The Rat-Pit* (1915) and *Moleskin Joe* (1923) are classics in the literary canon of Irish migration to Scotland. They portray a gritty and, at times, harum-scarum lifestyle based on early events in MacGill's own experience. By various turns he was a casual farm worker, drainer, hammer-man, navvy, plate-layer, tramp and wrestler. He was born in 1890 in Glenties, one of the wilder parts of Donegal, the eldest of a family of ten. By the age of 14 he had embarked on life as a farmhand with a seasonal tattie squad travelling on and off to Scotland for the next seven years. His early novels were re-published by Caliban, London, in the 1980s and also Edinburgh publishers, Birlinn.

91 O Ciarain, 1991, 79–80. Compare MacGill's equally vivid description of women working at the potato lifting in *Children of the Dead End* (1983 reprint, 75). See also reminiscences of Midlothian tattie lifters in MacDougall, 1995.

92 Fenton, 1976, 121 (and photograph opposite showing squad with gaffers and potato barrels).

93 Imrie, 1990, 27.

94 Fenton, 1976, 121–23 (and photograph on page 57). Tattie pits with stone-lined entrances resembling small souterrains have been preserved at Glenesk, Angus. See also photograph of a potato 'clamp' at Newburgh, Fife in 1958 in the evocatively captured selections of rural life found in the photographs of John P. Munn, Munn, *c.* 2005, 99.

95 Imrie, 1990, 27.

96 Sybil Berrecloth quoted in 'The Craigie' column of *The Courier*, Friday 15 June, 2012.

97 7 Hawkhill, Dundee, and other branches throughout the city of Dundee. Formerly J. Murdoch Wallace at 108 Mount Pleasant in Dundee City Directory 1946–47.

98 Hodge, 1921.

99 Trade Directories for Blairgowrie in the period 1897 to 1930 do not list fruit 'Merchants'. Messrs Keay & Hodge, Wellmeadow are listed as solicitors as early as 1897. J. M. Hodge appears as Clerk to the Burgh of Rattray from as early as 1901, and is listed as a Justice of the Peace for Blairgowrie District in Slater's Directory of 1921.

100 In 1902 after the Essendy estate was bought by a syndicate, it was their intention to replace the so-called 'tramp' labour with respectable pickers. Application for female pickers was made to the Scottish Council for Women's Trades and the

Salvation Army. Four hundred certified women were hired along with 300 boys from two industrial schools in Glasgow. The industrial boys surpassed expectations by picking nearly 100 tons in a month. *The Friend*, 16 November 1906.

Women came from a wide range of occupations: textile workers, dressmakers, milliners, shop assistants, teachers, clerks, mantle-makers and employees in rubber, confectionary, bookbinding, fancy box factories, as well as domestic servants. In 1903 there were reportedly 107 fruit growers in the Blairgowrie district, farming 520 acres. *Glasgow Herald*, 17 June 1905.

Hodge, 1921, 67–87 has a good deal of information about pickers as well as vintage photographs that include one of industrial schoolchildren going to work (p.80). By 1918 fruit growers were expected to recruit pickers from the local labour exchange. Cheap rail fares in the form of vouchers could be obtained. The berry harvest was deemed vital for the armed services and the nation as a whole in the First World War.

101   The long-established grower at the Welton, Mr James M. McDonald, was the first to recognise the need for seasonal housing for pickers. 'He erected corrugated iron buildings, fitted with wooden beds, and supplied with straw and blankets.' Hodge, 1921, 16.

102   *Evening Telegraph*, 20 April 1906.

103   *Blairgowrie Advertiser*, 18 July 1903.

104   *Evening Telegraph*, 22 July 1903.

105   The booking clerk at the railway station was required to sign and date the certificate.

106   Dormitories or cubicles slept six to 14 people and could be reserved with due notice. Parties had to bring blankets and their own cooking utensils by this time (*c.*1950s), although there was a nearby shop and also numerous vans calling at the farm. There was, however, no canteen. A hot plate was provided for cooking.

107   In January 1939 the workforce at Gothens consisted of grieve (Dick O'Neil) who was paid cash wages of fifty shillings plus perks of house, mill and meal, along with a pig, thirty hens and coals; tractor-man (Norman Hay), foreman (John Wallace), second (Dudley Campbell), fruit 'gaffer' (William Whyte), cattleman (Charles McGregor) and two casual workers paid at eightpence an hour for the male and sixpence an hour for the female. All employees got accommodation plus perks of a lesser extent than that of the grieve.

1939 also saw the number of camps on the moor estimated at about seventy in mid-July with a seasonal workforce of 350. Those camping were referred to as the 'Moor Squad' and their numbers could fluctuate. Pickers who served notice by post of their intention to work had to fill in a rudimentary form which was returned to the farm manager. There was a fee of one shilling for this registration.

108   Wolfhill is a village six and a half miles NE of Perth that formerly had pendicles.

109   As their traditional craft skills found less of a market amongst the buying public, Travellers had to diversify into casual farm work especially from the 1930s onwards. An idea of this diversity of skills is provided by Stanley Robertson:

'Dry-hunting was a means of getting things for little or nothing and they would sell them to whoever required the commodities. In the summer months, they would gather the fruit harvests and later the potatoes. The womenfolk would sell perfumes and scrubbers that they made from nature. These women were also very psychic and they told fortunes to people at markets and fairs.' Robertson, S. in Beech et al, 2005, 314.

The Travellers of Scotland did such work as gathering pine cones, picking clover-stones from the fields, turnip shawing, helping with the grain and potato harvests, as well as berry picking. Farmers were happy to employ them. In return the Travellers were afforded a place to camp and families often pooled their resources. They frequented old established fairs and markets such as the Fair o Blair held on the Tuesday following the fourth Monday of July.

110   See Borthwick, 1939. New edition, 1947, 90–104. See Obituary of Alastair Borthwick (1919–2003) in the *Daily Telegraph*, 19 March 2003.

111   Burkers in Traveller tradition ought not to be confused with resurrectionists or grave-robbers. The Burkers were doctors and their accomplices (often medical students) who snatched victims off lonely roads or at isolated camps. They wanted fresh bodies. Their mode of transport was a horse-drawn coach. Hooves were padded and in some stories bloodhounds loped alongside ready to sniff out potential victims for the mortuary slab. Deserted farm buildings made convenient temporary morgues for the Burkers until they could reach the dissecting rooms of the day.

112   Alexander Stewart. See Leitch, 1988, 51–52. The larger extract quoted herein conveys the atmosphere and revelry.

113   Adverts for employing berry-pickers in the 1930s were placed in a variety of newspapers: *Glasgow Evening News* and *Glasgow Evening Times*, *People's Journal* (Dundee edn) *Alloa Journal*, *Stirling Journal* and *Glasgow Citizen*. An example is: 'Fruitpickers wanted for ensuing season; dormitory accommodation free. Special arrangements for small parties. Apply Manager, Gothens Farm, Blairgowrie.' In the Hodge Archive of files and scrapbook cuttings are incoming letters from fruitpickers (usually women writing) for 1957–69.

114   I recorded Mrs Margaret Miller in August 2011 at Blairgowrie, where she had moved with her husband who was grieve at Gothens. Mrs Miller was a Dundonian. Sadly, she passed away in September 2014.

115   Bill Anderson's father had been a policeman stationed in Blairgowrie for a second time in 1966. Bill Anderson worked on Easter Essendy Farm as a gaffer for the MacAskill's where he oversaw a squad bussed in each day from Scone. Recorded in St Andrews on 16 November 2014.

'It was very busy at night. My dad was very busy sortin out the pubs cos they'd something like 18 pubs in Blair at that time and that's when he spent most of his time. And young lads like us, we didnae go down to the Wellmeadow [laughs] cos there were tensions between Dundee folk and Glasgow folk and they would come in. They would maybe stay at Essendy and they would come in for a drink on a night.'

116   Hamish Henderson collected untapped riches during fieldwork trips at this time. He writes:

'At camp fires in the berryfields of Blairgowrie, in council houses at Perth, and in the heart of secret-looking woodlands in the Mearns (an ancestral hideout) members of the Travelling fraternity, young and old, sang rare Child ballads, lyric love songs, execution broadside ballads, kids' rhymes, contemporary pop songs, you name it, they sang it. The only trouble (if you can call it trouble) was that everyone sang, or wanted to sing, right down to the smallest children.' Henderson, H. 'The Ballad, The Folk and the Oral Tradition' in Cowan, 1991, 80.

117   Maurice Fleming worked with Hamish Henderson in collecting at the berry-fields. See 'Songs and Ballads from Perthshire', Greentrax CD, Scottish Traditions, vol. 24.

118   See Henderson, H. 'The Ballad, The Folk and the Oral Tradition' in Cowan, 1991, 81.

119   'Once he had his pails filled, the picker makes for the weigh-in point at the edge of the field. At the beginning around Blairgowrie, payment was made of two shillings to two shillings sixpence a day, but many grumbled that they were given heavier drills to pick than other neighbours, so piecework was introduced, origi-nally at a halfpence per pound for all berries. Cheques were given at the weigh-in, cashable each evening, but since this obliged the growers to work an extra one and a half hours a night, payment by the pail or punnet, at a rate per pound, was substituted after only a few days.' J. R. Baldwin, 'The Berries', *Scots Magazine*, October, 1972, 13.

120   *Antwerp* was a type of raspberry popular at the time.

121   Betsy Whyte, a well-respected Traveller and author, mentions strikes started by the settled pickers in the first volume of her autobiography:

'Sometimes they would start strikes and marches from one berry farm to another, getting all the other berry pickers to strike as well. During these strikes they sometimes played havoc with farmers' property: burning fencing posts and even hayricks and cutting the telephone wires, lest the farmer should phone the police. We wanted no part of this, but we were forced to stay away from work under threat.' Whyte, 2001 edn, 108.

Firebrand poacher, Dugald Munro, falsified his age at 14 years to sign up to the army in the First World War and became a private, later a corporal. He wrote about the mass unemployment in Dundee and how 'the unemployed went to gather potatoes at one shilling and sixpence a day. Failing that they went to the 'berries' to earn a few miserable shillings.' He states that the pickers were cheated and short weighed by some farmers. 'Any trouble and you were put off the fields and blacklisted.' The arrival of the man with the wee black bag – the hated Means Test man – could clear the dreels of pickers in case their benefits were cut after being before the courts for fraud. Munro, 1975, 14.

122 See 'Berry Buses and Tattie Transport' in MacDonald, 2006, 57–68. Most of the vehicles came from the bus company Alexander or were former corporation vehicles. The matriarch of the Souter transport dynasty was the late Cathie Souter (1912–2006). For two decades she organised berry-picking buses from the Letham housing estate in Perth to Blairgowrie, supervising and overseeing over 100 berry pickers, many of whom were children. See also, 'Cathie Souter – an appreciation', *The Scotsman*, 7 June 2006

123 Packed to the brim: stowed out.

124 A definition of nabble in the *SND* is 'of workers in a cloth-making factory: to work fast in getting threads together'. When they nabble they are working speedily.

125 In 1946 soft fruit was dispatched by rail from Blairgowrie to jam manufacturers across the UK. This included the six outlets of: Co-operative Wholesale Society (CWS) mainly to New Middleton Junction; Hartley's of London, Hereford, and Aintree also took large tonnages; Keiller's of Dundee; Roberston's of Manchester; and T. G. Tickler's of Grimsby also feature in records amongst the Hodge papers.

    The earlier decades of the twentieth century saw considerable freight traffic in soft fruit leaving Blairgowrie. For one day a special fruit train comprised of 49 wagons carrying 100 tons. *Blairgowrie Advertiser*, 14 August 1909. The subject of fruit traffic by rail is covered by an excellent and well-researched article by 'Tales from the Berry Train' in *The True Line*, **141**, (July 2018), 32–43. This article reveals freight statistics previously unpublished from the J. M. Hodge Archival Collection. In the peak year of 1909 the seven weeks of the berry season saw 2600 tons of raspberries despatched from the station at Blair.

126 The Caledonian Railway Company was not well endowed with suitable freight wagons, although they did have them. 'Meat vans, covered carriage trucks, full brake vans and other stock having adequate means of ventilation were utilised.' Brenchley, 2018, 32–43.

127 'Down in the neck' – indicating the jam wasn't filled up to the required level.

128 Wordie & Co, based at Blairgowrie Railway Station, was a long-established firm of carters. They appear in local Trades' Directories from as far back as 1885 under carting contractors, Wordie & Co., Tannage Street. Their sentinel steam lorries with trailer-loaded wooded barrels of raspberries for pulp can be seen in Brenchley, T. 'Blairgowrie' *British Railway Journal*, **41**, 63. Prior to 1915 most of the crop was despatched in this way. A small amount of high-grade fruit was packed in punnets. See also, Brenchley, 2018, 32–43.

129 Prior to this there had been the Perthshire Constabulary, Angus Constabulary and the City of Dundee Police.

130 Marlee Hotel and farm, Blairgowrie.

131 Similarly at Gothens Farm there was an on-site policeman, as Andrew Hodge recalled:

'I mean before the war – things have changed a lot – if somebody was caught on the farm, say stealing potatoes, there was a room on the farm where they were put in the clink, just a wee room with a locked door, as punishment. Probably by the policeman who was employed over the summer months … . They thought nothing of it. There was no rights, no lawyer and before the Second World War that was quite common. That room still exists, not used obviously!'

For 1943, a typescript of the policeman's duties can be found in the J. M. Hodge papers. He was to keep order generally at the farm steading where pickers were located and, as far as possible, prevent the hooligan element interrupting work or vandalising farm property.

132   For 1966 two hotels are listed in the Trades Directory as being in the Wellmeadow, Blairgowrie. There were also three pubs with licences given. This is probably not comprehensive as there was no obligation to be listed in such a directory and there was a fee for inclusion. *Dundee, Angus and Perth Trades' Directory*, 1966. (Town and County Directories Ltd, Edinburgh), under 'Blairgowrie'.

133   See Walker, 1976, 92–93 for the historical background to burgh courts. Better still is Walker, 1995, 332, 335, 342, 420.

134   Accused persons on a snapshot of one day in July, 1909, found those before the Police Court were designated as 'ploughmen', 'berrypickers', 'labourers', 'house-wife', 'tinker' and 'pedlar'. Most appeared on drink-related minor offences such as creating a disturbance. The local newspaper took to using the abbreviation, 'b' in respect of berry pickers, such was their frequency before the Police Court.

135   See Borthwick, 1939. The author's rather nostalgic book refers to the 1930s.

136   PP Cd.8731.

137   Correspondence from William P. Smith, Blairgowrie, 17 April 1906, pasted into scrapbook 2, J. M. Hodge Archive. The actual number was thought to be even greater.

138   A term from South Africa for a hut village (especially one surrounded by a stockade) or enclosure for livestock.

139   Captain P. Laurence Oliphant, author of *The Tramp* (1913), PP Cd.8731.

140   Hodge Archives, scrapbook cutting.

141   Hodge Archives, scrapbook cutting.

142   Ruth Wishart quoted one woman who thought she was 'a snob' for bringing rugs and colourful bedcovers to the camp. Wishart, R. 'Berry Picking But Still Bites Down on the Farm Work Camp', *Scotsman Magazine*, 18 August 1984.

143   O'Neill, 1996, 40. Mrs D__. One of 15 siblings, she left school aged 14 and worked as a casual labourer and factoryhand.

144   According to PP Cd.6894, Vol. xxi, 11, most migratory workers from Ireland came from the province of Connaught. Out of these, two-thirds were from County Mayo, particularly the island of Achill.

145   Achill is one of the principal islands off the coast of Mayo. At the turn of the nineteenth century it had a population of over 4600. Nearly all able-bodied men and unmarried women left for work on farms in Scotland and England between April and July, though many remained away for three-quarters of each year. PP Cd.6894, Vol. xxi, 57. See also Revd P. J. Joyce, 'Irish Girl Migrants' *Irish Independent*, 3 February 1920, 4, which refers to MacGill's novel, *The Rat-Pit* failing to remove the scandal of living conditions in 'cowsheds'. Achill Island was a main outward migration area and in 1905 the number of migrants to

Scotland from there was put at between 1500 and 1600. Handley, 1943, 291–92.

146 Bell, 1991, 76–77.

147 Housing conditions for these workers and the legislation surrounding them, with particular reference to the nineteenth century, has been documented by Heather Holmes. See Holmes, H. 'Housing for Seasonal Agricultural Workers' in Stell et al, 2007, 237–39, 242.

148 Thorne, 1991, 76. An interesting parallel can be made with French Canadians who travelled to Maine in family groups in order to do the potato picking. They travelled over the border for the harvest season, sleeping in trucks and trailers or tents. Steinbeck puts them into a category of migrant crop-picking people from a diversity of origins in the USA: Hindus, Filipinos, Mexicans and Okies. See Steinbeck, 2000, 50–55.

149 O'Dowd, 1991.

150 Melville, 1939, 42. This was more true of the Earn.

151 NAS. AF 56/1422. Report by Alexander Carmichael, 'Fishing Lodges on the Tay and Earn', 11 May 1889.

152 In George Orwell's thinly disguised fiction about the hop picking in Kent the importance of the mobile 'shops' is brought to the fore. See Orwell, 1935.

153 The old costerwoman mentioned in Orwell's *A Clergyman's Daughter*, London, 1935, had her songs too as there are parallels with the hop picking and other cultures. The pickers never grew tired of singing them; they must have sung both of them several hundred times over before the season came to an end. As much a part of the atmosphere of the hopfields as the bitter scent and the blowsy sunlight were the tunes of these two songs, ringing through the leafy lanes of the times.

154 Henderson, 2004, 102.

155 Or conyach, the ability to combine words, melody and delivery into a single, moving spirit.

156 See McKean and Whatley, 2008, especially 126–27.

157 See McKenzie, 1987, where the lens of art photographer, Joseph McKenzie, artistically succeeds in capturing the last vestiges of people and place as the bulldozers moved into the area.

158 Sinderins connected the bottom of Blackness Avenue and Perth Road to Hawkhill. Gillian Molloy explains it is from the Scots word scinder, to part, in Molloy, 2019, 101.

159 See Crumley, 1996, 111–25.

160 Only Aberdeen had a lower proportion of houses having exclusive use of a toilet. Dundee had, in 1951, the lowest proportion of households having a fixed bath in any of the four Scottish cities of that time. Jackson, 1979, 369

161 A sink was sometimes referred to as the 'jaw box'. See Coogan with Ogilvy, 2012, 17. The author washed at the sink when a student in the 1970s. He shared a basement tenement flat with no bathroom and an outside WC. The rent was £12 per week between three occupants.

162 'The vast majority of households had exclusive use of a piped water supply, kitchen sink and kitchen stove.' The figure was between 90 and 95 per cent in 1951. Jackson, 1979, 368.

163　The *Dundee City Directory* for 1946–47 gives the address for Guthrie Street Baths and Washing House as 21 Guthrie Street. This listing did not appear in the 1973 edition of the directory.

164　The Society of St Vincent de Paul was established in Scotland in 1833 and is still active.

165　Kay, 1996, 43.

166　Wm G. Dickson, 28 Westport. The only pawnshop listed in the *Dundee City Directory* for 1973. See Clark and Carnegie 2003, 75, 153–54. Dickson the pawnbrokers is listed as having three premises in the *Dundee City Directory* for 1946–47, one of five such businesses listed in the city at that time.

167　Pipe clay was formerly used for whitening the stairs of tenement properties, rubbed over the wet stairs to dry out whiter. Cleaning was often organised by a rota of the neighbours. (If a householder forgot, a mop handle might be put through their letter box as a direct reminder.) See Faley, 2005, 93–96.

168　See Faley, 2005, 53–55 for the children's contribtions to tenement living.

169　'I usetae stay at my granny's and she stayed in Lochee and I usetae get the berry bus every morning at six o'clock without fail … . Ye didna make much money but ye always had to hand it over to your mother to pay for your school clothes. We were brought up as slaves. You think I'm jokin. Every penny got took off us. Aye. [Clothes] were hand-me-downs. Everything was handed down. Paul Hill (b.1962) recorded by Roger Leitch on 29 October 2014. See also Clark and Carnegie, 2010, 156–58.

170　Draffens was a department store in the Nethergate which opened in 1934 and closed in the early 1980s.

171　Broth, soup made with vegetables, with or without the addition of meat. Frequently prefixed by the name of the principal ingredient, as meal(y)-kail, *SND*.

172　In other parts of Scotland, such as Paisley and Edinburgh, informants mention soup being a staple in their diet. Cheaper cuts of meat and homegrown vegetables were used in the household of an Edinburgh civil servant in the 1950s and early 60s. Both parents worked hard in the vegetable garden growing tatties, onions, neeps, small white turnips, lettuce, carrots, peas, beans and also rhubarb. The Co-op in Blackhall was regularly used and the fisherwife from Newhaven going from house to house with her creel, along with the Onion Johnny on his bicycle, were kenspeckle figures in 1950s Edinburgh. Information from interviews with Irene Lodge and Sylvia Robertson.

173　Other people corroborate the routine of meals such as mince, stews, potted hough and liver. Bread as a staple might be bought every second day.

174　Harry Wallace, piebaker, 155A Wilkie's Lane, Hawkhill (1963). Wallace's pie shop was a Dundee institution.

175　Dundee stovies were usually made with corned beef. In urban west Scotland they were sausage baked, with sliced onions and potatoes in both areas. The more affluent might use remains of a pot roast.

176　Sylvia Robertson recalled Christmas lunch as being 'a huge treat' with chicken soup followed by roast hen and homemade Christmas pudding:

'One of my father's sisters always sent a hen from the farm in Banffshire – a box wrapped in brown paper (with strong sealing wax) and inside a fresh plucked hen swathed in greaseproof paper. In with the hen, neatly tucked down the side, a currant bun, the speciality of one of the Banff bakers, absolute heaven sliced and buttered!'

177   First-foot – the first person to enter a home on New Year's day.

178   Chips and peas smothered in vinegar, so called because of its flatulence-inducing properties *SND*.

179   See Reynolds, 2007 reprint, 14. This references the 'dozens and dozens of barrows selling everything from hooters and hats to fancy-dressed herrings'.

180   It was New Queen's College and part of St Andrews University until 1967 when the University of Dundee received its Royal Charter. See Shafe, 1982, 202.

181   Undergraduate law degree.

182   The author recalls 'The Tav' being an arty place to be in the early 1970s, heaving with folk and a roaring coal fire. Patrons could be five or six deep at the bar. At 147 Hawkhill the pub was very popular with students. It survived until 1976. The bar and fittings were relocated to the Dundee University Students Union. Alexander, 1992, 19.

183   8 North Tay Street.

184   Micky Coyle joined the Dundee Wine, Spirit and Beer Trade Protection Association in 1893 and his MC Rum was extremely popular, with or without a cold. Alexander, 1992, 47.

185   Until 1960 it was only legal to bet in race courses, on the turf, which accounts for how plentiful bookies' runners were before this.

186   Coogan, 2012, 19. This is one of the most amazing life stories to emerge in recent years.

187   Caird (Dundee) Ltd, jute spinners and manufacturers, Ashton Works, 195 Hawkhill, (1946–47), later space dyers of carpets (1973).

188   See 'Weaving a Tale of Jute and Flax', *City Scene: Journal of the Dundee Civic Trust*, October 2014, *passim*. Colour photographs of the last extant lums of Dundee jute mills and factories, plus interesting articles.

189   See Faley, 2005, 28, 32, 58f, 59. The early twentieth-century four-roomed Glasgow tenement restored by the National Trust for Scotland retains authentic gas lighting to recreate the atmosphere. Electric lighting did not arrive until 1960.

190   From the age of eleven, girls did deliver milk and papers but these tended to be boys' jobs. See Clark and Carnegie, 2010, 45.

191   Robertson, 2009. Chapter 6, 'At the Berries' superbly evokes the spirit of the dreels in the 1960s.

192   Frank S. Laird, grocer, 66 Polepark Road.

193   The Mid Craigie scheme.

194   The Campbell's grandson, Andrew Wilson recalled (in conversation with Andrew Hodge) that his grandmother had come to Scotland from Achill Island. She picked tatties and berries in Perthshire and Angus and met Auchen when she

was picking tatties at Wellbank, Rattray for Andrew's uncle, J. M. Hodge. The pair married and Mary moved to Gothens where Auchen was already working. Andrew remembers Auchen with great affection:

'[Auchen] took a great interest in the Bronze-Age flints and arrowheads that surfaced when the farm land was cultivated. In retirement, he kept the kitchen garden for my parents and I well remember him digging up worms to allow me to go fishing in the nearby Lunan Burn.'

GLOSSARY

bummer	a factory mill siren
coble	a small flat-bottomed rowing boat, used mostly in river or lake fishing, or for salmon fishing by nets near the coast, *SND*
fee'd	engaged as a farm servant/employment
janker	a device for transporting logs
gelly	type of tent constructed by Travellers
gralloch/ gralloching	the entrails of a deer, which are removed as soon as possible after the deer has been killed
grilse	a salmon that has returned to fresh water after a single winter at sea
karabiner	metal clip used in mountaineering
kebbuck heel	the last remaining hard-end of a cheese, *SND*
luggie	a berry pail, bucket
pally	a close, friendly relationship
pannie	chores such as preparing kindling or porridge in the farm bothy
penny vantis	soft drink
pletty	open-air communal landing at the back of a block of tenement flats
sculls	a shallow scoop-shaped oval basket of wicker, wooden laths or wire mesh, used for carrying peats, turnips, potatoes, grain or the like, *SND*

NOTE:
A useful reference to words in the Dundonian Scots can be found in Norman Lynn's book, *The Dundee Row Laddie No 2*, (n.p. 1982), pp.115–17.

CONTRIBUTORS

Andy Anderson, b.1957
Bill Anderson, b.1948
Mike Anderson, b.1963
Mary Angus, b.1940
John Barrie, b.1912
John H. Beaton MBE,
 b.1937
Jackson Bett, b.1908
Andrew Bruce, b.1913
Jenny Burns, b.1963
John Cameron
Willie Cameron
Jock Christie, b.1900
Sarah Craig
Bernadette Dailly, b.1954
Douglas Davidson, b.1928
Jim Davidson, b.1934
Jim Devlin, b.1933
Therese Devlin, b.1957
David Dick, b.1908
Diane Donnelly, b.1934
Andy Fenwick, b.1964
Bob Fotheringham, b.1945
Irene Fyfe, b.1940
Maureen Gardiner, b.1936
Wull Halliday
Heather Hay, b.1957
John Henderson, b.1925
Mike Henderson, b.1963
Paul Hill, b.1962

Andrew Hodge, b.1958
Helen Jackson, b.1915
Tom Jarvis Jnr, b.1936
Tib Johnstone, b. c.1914
John Jordan, b.1948
Helen Kay, b.1907
Sandy Kay, b.1900
Joan Kettles, b.1954
Henry Kinnaird, b.1913
Alex Lackie, b.1957
Tom Logie, b.1904
Anne McDonald, b.1946
Donald MacDonald of
 Eriskay, b.1912
Donald A. MacDonald,
 b.1929
Willie MacFarlane, b.1954
Mike Macfarlane, b.1956
Andy McKay, b.1940
James McLaren, b.1912
Margaret McMaster,
 b.1958
Jock Mcpherson, b.1936
Maureen Marra, b.1949
George Mathieson
Brian Melville, b.1956
Chic Milne, b.1923
Margaret Miller, b.1931
Jock Mollinson, b.1908
Angus Morrison b.1925

Ian Murray, b.1941
Bill Nicol, b.1912
Jim Ogg, b.1906
Anne Piggott, b.1939
Cecil Prowie, b.1913
Ian J. Robertson, b.1952
Jim Robertson, b.1932
Sylvia Robertson
John Scobie, b.1920
Stanley Sim, b.1928
David Sinclair CBE,
 b.1922
Iain Smart, b.1949
Duncan Soutar, b.1946
Jonathan Stansfeld MBE
John Stewart, b.1946
Sandy Stewart, b.1920
Peggie Stewart, b.1925
Sheila Stewart MBE,
 b.1935
Dean Tait, b.1962
Peter Taylor, b.1900
Prof. Derick S. Thomson,
 b.1921
Joe Tindall, b.1916
Sheena Wellington,
 b.1944
Bob Wilson, b.1926
David Wilson, b.1937

BIBLIOGRAPHY

Alexander, John. *Dundee Pubs, Past and Present.* John Alexander/Urban
    Printers, Dundee, 1992.

Beech, John et al (eds). *The Individual in Community Life,* vol. 9, Scottish
    Life and Society: A Compendium of Scottish Ethnology. John Donald,
    Edinburgh, 2005.

Bell, Jonathan 'Donegal Women as Migrant Workers in Scotland', *ROSC* 7
    (1991).

Bennett, Margaret (ed.). *Recollections of an Argyllshire Drover and other West
    Highland Chronicles by Eric R. Cregeen.* Grace Note Publications,
    Ochtertyre, 2013.

Borthwick, Alastair. *Always a Little Further.* Eneas Mackay, Stirling, 1939.

Brenchley, T. 'Tales from the Berry Train' in *The True Line,* **141**, (July 2018).

Carmichael, Alexander 'Fishing Lodges on the Tay and Earn', 1889.

Cheape, Hugh and Sprott, Gavin. *Angus Country Life: a Companion to the
    Angus Folk Museum.* Glamis, Edinburgh, 1980.

Clark, Helen and Carnegie, Elizabeth. *She Was Aye Workin: Memories of
    Tenement Women in Edinburgh and Glasgow.* White Cockade and The
    People's Palace, Glasgow City Council, Dorchester, 2003.

Collins English Dictionary.

Concise Scots Dictionary.

Coogan, Andy with Ogilvy, Graham. *Tomorrow You Die: The Astonishing
    Story of a Second World War Prisoner of the Japanese.* Mainstream,
    Edinburgh and London, 2012.

Cowan, Edward J. (ed.). *The People's Past,* Polygon, Edinburgh, 1991.

Crumley, Jim. *The Road and the Miles: A Homage to Dundee.* Mainstream,
    Edinburgh and London, 1996.

Delargy, James. *The Gaelic Story-Teller with some Notes on Gaelic Folk Tales,*
    [Sir John Rhys Memorial Lecture], Reprinted from *Proceedings of the
    British Academy,* Vol. XXXI. London, Cumberlege, 1945.

Devine, T. M. 'Temporary Migration and the Scottish Highlands in the Nineteenth Century', *The Economic History Review* (2) **32**, 1979.

Devine, T. M. *The Scottish Clearances: A History of the Dispossessed, 1600–1900.* Penguin, London, 2019.

Dickson, J. 'The Agriculture of Perthshire', *Transactions of the Highland Society*, II (1868–69).

Dorson R. M. (ed.). *Folkore and Folklife An Introduction.* The University of Chicago Press, 1972.

Dostoevsky, Fyodor (translated by Constance Garnett). *The House of the Dead* and *The Gambler.* Wordsworth Classics, Ware, 2010.

Douglas, Robert. *Night Song of the Last Tram.* Hodder & Stoughton, London, 2005.

Douglas, Graham and Oglethorpe, Miles. K. *Brick, Tile and Fireclay Industries in Scotland.* RCAHMS, Edinburgh, 1993.

Faley, Jean. *Up Oor Close: Memories of Domestic Life in Glasgow Tenements, 1910–1945.* White Cockade in association with Springburn Museum Trust, Glasgow, 2005.

Fenton, A. (ed.). *At Brechin with Stirks: a farm cashbook from Buskhead, Glenesk, Angus, 1885–1898.* Birlinn, Edinburgh, 1994.

Fenton, Alexander and Veitch, Kenneth. (eds). *Farming and the Land*, vol. 2, Scottish Life and Society: A Compendium of Scottish Ethnology. John Donald, Edinburgh, 2005.

Fenton, Alexander. *Scottish Country Life.* John Donald, Edinburgh, 1976.

Gray, Affleck. *The Big Grey Man of Ben Macdhui.* Impulse Books, Aberdeen, 1970.

Groome's Ordnance Gazetteer, (new edition), vol 1, *c.*1891.

Handley, James E. *The Irish in Scotland*, Cork University Press, Cork, 1943.

Hay, Edna R. and Walker, Bruce. *Focus on Fishing: Arbroath and Gourdon.* Abertay Historical Society publication 23, Dundee, 1985.

Henderson, Hamish (Finlay, Alec, ed.). *Alias MacAlias, Writings on Songs, Folk and Literature.* Polygon, Edinburgh, 2004.

Hodd, Adrian N. L. 'Agricultural Change in the Carse of Gowrie, 1750–1875', PhD thesis, University of Dundee, 1974.

Hodge, J. M. *Raspberry Growing in Scotland.* The Scottish Smallholders Organisation Ltd, Edinburgh, 1921.

Hume, John, R. *The Industrial Archaeology of Scotland*, 2 vols, vol. 1: *The Lowlands and Borders.* Harper Collins, London, 1976.

Imrie, Dan. *Around the Farms, 1930s & 40s.* Privately printed, Glenrothes, 1990.

Ives, Sandy. *The Tape-Recorded Interview*. The University of Tennessee Press, Knoxville, 1974.

Jackson, J. M. (ed.). 'Housing in the City of Dundee,' *Third Statistical Account of Scotland*. The Herald Press, Arbroath, 1979, 362–85.

Johnston's Gazetteer of Scotland, 2nd edition, 1958.

Kay, Billy (ed.). *The Complete Odyssey: Voices from Scotland's Recent Past*. Birlinn, Edinburgh, 1996.

Kerr, John. *The Living Wilderness: Atholl Deer Forests*. Jamieson and Munro, Perth, 1986.

Leitch, Roger. *The Book of Sandy Stewart*, Scottish Academic Press, Edinburgh, 1988.

Leitch, Roger. *By Bicycle in Scotland: cycle-touring on the quiet roads of Scotland*. Impact Books, London, 1993.

MacDonald, Donald Archie. *Ugan Agus Bhuam (To Me and From Me)*. Club Leabhar, Stornoway, 1977.

MacDonald, Douglas G. *Saved from the Scrapyard: Scottish Buses Recycled*. The History Press, Stroud, 2006.

MacDougall, Ian. *Hard Work Ye Ken: Midlothian Women Farmworkers*, Flashback series. EERC/Midlothian Council, Edinburgh, 1993.

MacDougall, Ian. *Hoggie's Angels: Tattie Howkers Remember*. Flashback series. Midlothian Council, Edinburgh, 1995.

MacDougall, Ian. *Through the Mill: Personal Recollections by veteran men and women Penicuik Paper Mill Workers*. The Scottish Working People's History Trust, Falkirk, 2009.

MacDougall, Ian. *Voices of Scottish Journalists*. The Scottish Working People's History Trust/John Donald, Edinburgh, 2013.

MacGill, Patrick. *Children of the Dead End*. Caliban Books, London, 1983.

MacGill, Patrick. *The Rat-Pit*. Caliban Books, London, 1983.

MacGill, Patrick. *Moleskin Joe*. Birlinn, Edinburgh, 2000.

McIlvanney, William. *The Kiln*. Canongate Books, Edinburgh, 2014.

McKean, Charles and Whatley, Patricia with Baxter, Kenneth. *Lost Dundee: Dundee's Lost Architectural Heritage*. Birlinn, Edinburgh, 2008.

McKenzie, Joseph. *Pages of Experience: Photography 1947–1987*. Polygon and the Third Eye Centre, Edinburgh and Glasgow, 1987.

Mackenzie, Osgood H. *A Hundred Years in the Highlands*. Birlinn, Edinburgh, 1995.

Maclean, Calum I. *The Highlands*, Club Leabhar, Inverness, 1975.

Martin, Angus. *Herring Fishermen of Kintyre and Ayrshire*, House of Lochar, Argyll, 2002.

Martin, Angus. *The Larch Plantation*. Macdonald, Loanhead, 1990.

Melville, Lawrence. *The Fair Land of Gowrie*, William Culross & Son Ltd, Coupar Angus, 1939.

Michie, Margaret F. with Fenton, Alexander and Beech, John (eds). *Glenesk: The History and Culture of an Angus Community*. Edinburgh, 2000.

Molloy, Gillian. *Street names of Old Dundee*. Friends of Dundee City Archives, Dundee, 2019.

Morrison, Dorothy and Reynolds, Isobel. *Rural Schools in Angus*. Pinkfoot Press, Brechin, 2004.

Munn, John P., *Summers Lang Syne: Scotland 1930 to 1959*, (text by David Elliot), Falkirk Cultural Services, *c.*2005.

Munro, Dugald. *King of the Poachers*. David Winter & Son Ltd, Dundee, 1975.

Murphy, Michael J. *Tyrone Folk Quest*. Blackstaff Press, Belfast, 1973.

Neat, Timothy. *When I Was Young: Voices From Lost Communities In Scotland: The Islands*. Birlinn, Edinburgh, 2000.

O Ciarain, Sean. *Farewell to Mayo: an emigrants memories of Ireland and Scotland*. Brookside, Dublin, 1991.

O'Dowd, Anne. *Spaleens and Tattie Hokers: History and Folklore of the Irish Migratory Agricultural Worker in Ireland and Britain*. Blackrock, Dublin, 1991.

O'Neill, Gilda. *Pull No More Bines: Hop Picking – Memories of a Vanished Way of Life*. The Women's Press Ltd, London, 1996.

Orr, Willie. *Deer Forests, Landlords and Crofters*. John Donald, Edinburgh, 1982.

Orwell, George. *A Clergyman's Daughter*. Victor Gollancz, London, 1935.

Oxford English Dictionary.

Penguin English Dictionary.

Reynolds, Maureen. *Voices in the Street: Growing up in Dundee*. Black and White Publishing, Edinburgh, 2007.

Robertson, Gary. *Skeem Life: Growing Up In The Seventies*. Black & White Publishing, Edinburgh, 2010.

Robertson, James C. *About St Andrews – And About*. J. & G. Innes, St Andrews, 1973.

Robertson, Willie. *On The Milk*. Hachette Scotland, London 2009.

Rothney, Stanley. 'Fly Francie Marks, the Wonderful Boy', *The Leopard*, (Sept 2011), 17–18.

Salmond, J. B. *Flower of the Flax*. Herbert Jenkins, London, 1944.

Satterley, Glyn. *Going to the Hill: Life on Scottish Sporting Estates*. Quiller Press Ltd, Shrewsbury, 2012.

Scottish National Dictionary (*SND*), https://dsc.ac.uk.

Shafe, Michael (comp.). *University Education in Dundee 1881–1981: A Pictorial*

History. University of Dundee, Dundee, 1982.

Smout, T. C. *A Century of the Scottish People, 1830–1950.* Wm Collins & Sons, London, 1986.

Smout, T. C. *Scotland and the Sea.* John Donald, Edinburgh, 1992.

Smout, T. C, and Wood, Sydney. *Scottish Voices 1745–1960*, Wm Collins & Sons, London, 1990.

Steinbeck, John. *Travels with Charlie.* Penguin Classics, London, 2000.

Stell, Geoffrey, Shaw, John and Storrier, Susan (eds). *Scotland's Buildings*, A Compendium of Scottish Ethnology, vol 3. John Donald, Edinburgh, 2007.

Storrier, Susan, (ed.). *Scotland's Domestic Life*, vol. 6, Scottish Life and Society: A Compendium of Scottish Ethnology. John Donald, Edinburgh, 2006.

Symon, J. A. *Scottish Farming Past and Present.* Oliver and Boyd, Edinburgh and London, 1959.

Thomas, Dylan. *The Doctor and the Devils and other scripts by Dylan Thomas.* J. M. Dent & Sons, London, 1953.

Thomson, Derick S. (ed.). *The Companion to Gaelic Scotland.* Blackwell, Oxford, 1987.

Thorne, John, 'Donegal Women as Migrant Workers in Scotland', *ROSC* 7 (1991).

Walker, David M. *The Scottish Legal System: an Introduction to the Study of Scots Law.* W. Green and Son Ltd, Edinburgh, 1976.

Walker, David M. *A Legal History of Scotland: The sixteenth century, vol iii.* T. & T. Clark Ltd, Edinburgh, 1995.

Watson, Adam. *It's a Fine Day for the Hill.* Paragon, Northants, 2011.

Watson, Angus. *The Essential Gaelic-English English-Gaelic Dictionary*, Birlinn, Edinburgh, 2012.

Watson, Norman. *Dundee: A Short History*, Black and White Publishing, Edinburgh 2006.

Watson, Norman. *Poet McGonagall: The Biography of William McGonagall.* Birlinn, Edinburgh, 2010.

Watson, Norman. *The Dundee Dicshunury.* Forfar, 2011.

Whyte, Betsy. *The Yellow on the Broom.* Birlinn, Edinburgh, 1979, 2001.

Wylie, Thomas. *Logiealmond.* n.p., Perth, 1932.

Ziegler, Philip. *Britain Then & Now, The Francis Frith Collection.* Weidenfeld & Nicolson, London, 1999.

Newspapers and magazines:
Blairgowrie Advertiser.
The Courier (Dundee) (formerly *The Courier and Advertiser*).
Daily Telegraph.
Dundee Advertiser.
Evening Telegraph.
Glasgow Herald.
The Herald.
Leopard.
Perthshire Advertiser.
Scotland on Sunday magazine.
Scots Magazine.
The Scotsman.
Scotsman Magazine.
Irish Independent.

Directories:
Clark's Trades and Professions' Directory for Forfar, Perth and Fife, D. R. Clark
    and Son, Dundee, 1885.
Dundee City Directory.
Dundee, Forfar and Perth Trades' Directory, 1934–35.
Dundee City Directory, 1946–47.
Dundee, Forfar and Perth Trades' Directory, 1966.
Dundee City Directory, 1973.
Slater's Directory, 1921.

Journals:
British Railway Journal.
City Scene: Journal of the Dundee Civic Trust.
The Economic History Review.
Gairm.
The True Line. The Journal of the Caledonian Railway Association.
Proceedings of the British Academy.
ROSC: Review of Scottish Culture.
Tocher.
Transactions of the Highland Society, II (1868–69).

Logbooks:
Birnam School logbook 1874–1930.
Kinloch Rannoch School logbook 1937–81.
Royal Grammar School Dunkeld logbook, 1868–15 (January 1909).
Dunkeld School logbook 1915–30 (June 1916).

Parliamentary Papers (PP):
Eighteenth Annual Report of the Inspector of Salmon Fisheries for Scotland,
        Glasgow, 1899, Cd. 148.
Report of the Royal Commission on the Housing of the Industrial
        Population of Scotland: Rural and Urban. Edinburgh, 1917, Cd. 8731.
Royal Commission on Labour. The Agricultural Labourer (Ireland), vol. IV,
        pt IV, (1893–4), XXXVI, Cd. 6894, Vol. XXI.

Ordnance Survey Maps:
OS one-inch, Arbroath and Montrose, sheet 58, 1946.
OS one-inch to the mile, Perth and Strath Earn, sheet 63, 1927.

Other:
McGregor's Gathering, BBC Radio Scotland.
New Statistical Account X (1837).
Songs and Ballads from Perthshire, Greentrax CD, Scottish Traditions, vol. 24.

INDEX

* many informants may be talking about their experiences working as a child in the book; entries listed here are where they specifically mention working as a child.